Mustang at War

Mustang
at War

ROGER A. FREEMAN

Doubleday and Company, Inc.
GARDEN CITY, NEW YORK

Contents

'Dutch'

Introduction

There have been a number of publications about the North American Mustang and undoubtedly many more are to be expected of the aeroplane generally acknowledged as the best all-round fighter of the Second World War. The aim of this book is to give an appraisal of the Mustang throughout significant stages of its history and record opinions and recollections of some of those who built, flew and maintained this aircraft.

While a rounded account of a combat aeroplane must of necessity include technical aspects, specifications and tabulated data are not included in this attempt to convey to the reader the intrinsic qualities this aircraft was deemed to have by those who knew it well.

Some Allied and enemy contemporaries of the Mustang possessed advantages in some performance spheres, but were at definite disadvantages in others; whereas the Mustang did not fall far short on any aspect, whether at low-level or six miles high. Top speed in level flight, rate of climb and turning circle were generally held to be the most important factors in fighter performance and in these qualities the Merlin-engined Mustang did not lag. As fighter tactics evolved, the ability to overhaul an adversary in a dive or to pull away from him proved an even greater advantage; with its low-drag airframe the Mustang had few equals in dive performance. Able to more than hold its own with any interceptor, its crowning advantage was an endurance vastly superior to that of the single-seat fighters of its day.

The advanced design inherent in the Mustang can be directly attributed to the energy and drive of the manufacturers. Paradoxically, their very inexperience in fighter design aided the project by forcing a completely fresh approach in which the latest advances in aerodynamics were explored without bias or convention. North American's expeditious creation of this fighter was nothing short of remarkable.

Not all pilots viewed the Mustang as a joy to fly, but few failed to appreciate its prowess. Henri Pietrzak, a veteran Polish fighter ace and squadron commander with extensive experience in Merlin Mustangs, gave a succinct opinion that represents the views of the majority: 'The Mustang was an unforgiving aeroplane, but once understood and respected it was a superb fighter to handle.' From those who faced the Mustang as an enemy comes this compliment from Johannes Steinhoff, highly distinguished Luftwaffe commander and fighter pilot, 'That Mustang was *some* fighter!' It was.

ROGER A. FREEMAN

5

Acknowledgements

A book of this nature would not be possible without the recollections, records and souvenirs of many people connected in various ways with the Mustang. I express my grateful thanks to every one of them and hope that I have chronicled their contribution with truth and accuracy. John J. Sloan, Managing Editor of *AAHS Journal*, who worked on the prototype Mustang, was responsible for obtaining the reminiscences of Edgar Schmued, John Atwood and Bob Chilton. He also arranged for other historical material through the good offices of Earl Blount and Curtis Ruckdaschel of North American Rockwell. USAF agencies assisting were the Photographic Library of the Aerospace Audio Visual Service, through Mrs Virginia Finsic; USAF Office of Information, Washington, through Major Larry Brown; and Third Air Force Press Office where James Denmark and Vernon Burke went to great lengths to help. Other institutions I wish to thank are the South African National Museum of Military History, Public Archives of Canada, Public Records Office,

London, Negative Library of Royal Aircraft Establishment, East Anglian Aviation Society and the Imperial War Museum where Ted Hine and Geoffrey Pavy were of great assistance.

Michael Bowyer gave considerable guidance on RAF matters and Bruce Robertson gave advice and applied an editorial eye to the text. Contributors who provided information, anecdotes and illustrations so making this book possible are Dave Birch, Allan Blue, Richard Bateson, Frank Cheesman, Morris Curteis, Ken Clarkson, Mrs Diana Clover, Gerry Collins, Bob Dunnavant, Jeffrey Ethell, Stewart Evans, Tom Fazan, Garry Fry, Steve Gotts, Peter Hearne, George Kenning, Lew Nalls, Leroy Nitschke, Merle Olmsted, Alfred Price, Geoffrey Pleasance, Philip Pointz, Henri Pietrzak, Hans Ring, Charles Stover, Tadek Szymanski, Jesse Thompson, Raymond Veitch, Carl Vincent, Ron Williams and my good Dutch friend Gerrit Zwanenburg who, by alphabetical listing, is almost a certainty to round off the acknowledgements in books dealing with Second World War military aviation.

Bibliography

AF Combat Units of World War II Maurer Maurer (Dept. of AF)
Fighting Mustang William Hess (Doubleday)
Fighter Squadrons of the RAF John Rawlings (Macdonald)
Mustang: The Story of the P-51 Fighter R. W. Gruenhagen (Arco)

Photo Credits

Photographs in this book are from the following sources:—

North American Rockwell: 8, 9, 10, 11 and 12.
USAAF: 44, 53M, 54, 57, 58, 59, 60TR & LR, 62L, 63, 68, 70, 71T & M, 75, 90M, 99, 100TR, 101TR & LR, 102TL, 103T, 142TR, 146LL and 148T.
USAF: 40, 48, 49, 58T, 60TL, 61TR & TL, 64, 76, 77, 82, 84, 85, 91T, 92T, 98, 100TR & LR, 102L, 104T, 105M, 106M, 138, 142TL, 143TR, 144, 145, 146ML, 147T, 150, 153, 156 and 157.
Crown: 22T, 23, 26, 27, 29 & 36.
Public Archives of Canada: 32TL & TR, 33, 34, 35 & 37.
Imperial War Museum: 60LL, 62T, 100LL, 119, 134 & 135.
Air Force Museum: 55.
Rolls Royce Ltd: 51 & 53T.
RAE, Farnborough: 122.
Aeroplane: 21, 22M, 25TR & 28T.
Flight: 24 & 25L.
Impact: 146TR & 147M & L.
W. Barnes: 106L.
W. Blickenstaff: 93T.
R. Bowers: 71L.
Brewer: 96 & 104R.
S. Clay: 20, 28M & L, 30T, 31T & L, 106T, 116, 118, 120, 121, 126, 127, 130 & 154.
J. Cope: 90T.
M. Curties: 133 & 136.
R. Dunnavant: 159.
J. Ethell: 78, 88, 90L & 91L, 92L, 93L, 94, 95, 102TR, 103LR & LL.
P. Hearne: 131.
W. Larkins: 43 & 149L.
R. Little: 87.
G. Moriera: 142LR & 143LR.
L. Nitschke: 114 & 115.
M. Olmsted: 110, 111 & 112.
C. H. Stover: 32MR to LR.
T. Szymanski: 125.
J. Thompson: 104MR & 105M.
R. H. Veitch: 137.

The Twelve
Month Wonder

premium. Officially the United States had a policy of strict neutrality, although there was nothing to prevent a foreign nation from purchasing war material providing it was not actually engaged in hostilities at the time. Aircraft manufacturers in the United States had been leaders in some techniques of metal airframe construction and examples of their designs reaching Europe were much admired.

The British Air Commission made an extensive tour of all the major airframe and engine firms in the States and found that the majority were very willing to do business. The indigenous market for both civil and military aircraft was too limited to provide sufficient orders to sustain all the manufacturers in the field and only by securing export sales were some able to survive. Hence the British, generally, were very impressed by the initiative and drive of these companies, particularly Lockheed

LEADERS OF THE MUSTANG MAKERS
Top: 'Dutch' Kindelberger and John Atwood, President and Vice-President of North American.
Above right: Raymond Rice, Chief of Engineering.
Right: Edgar Schmued, Chief Design Engineer.
JUS' BEAU'FUL
Above: The NA-73X in flight and displaying the clean Mustang lines that became so famous.

In April 1938 the British Government sent an air commission to the United States to explore the possibilities of purchasing military aircraft. By this date the belligerent activities of Adolf Hitler had convinced most of Britain's military leaders that the nation would soon be drawn into a war with Nazi Germany. Intelligence sources revealed that an important part of Germany's rearmament was a powerful and very modern air arm and to counter this threat Britain was hastily expanding her Royal Air Force. But to train aircrews and build aircraft needed much time, and with one European crisis following hard upon another, time was undoubtedly at a and North American with plants in California. From Lockheed they ordered 200 reconnaissance bombers based on that company's successful transport and from North American a similar number of advanced trainers—the latter was in fact the first contract signed.

The North American trainer was basically a refined version of the firm's model that had obtained their initial production order from the US Army Air Corps in 1936. The British order, coming when it did, was the fillip that established North American as a major manufacturer and kept their Inglewood plant busily occupied for many months. The first Harvard—as the British version was named—was received in England for evaluation within four months of the contract being signed; prompt delivery in view of the long sea voyage from the west coast of the United States through the Panama Canal. The Harvard was found noisy, but otherwise a very stable and pleasant monoplane to fly. Its low wing configuration and general handling characteristics made it a good step for the trainee pilot headed for a single-seat fighter.

North American Aviation was originally incorporated as a holding company for the varied aviation interests of financier Clement Keys and his associates. The group acquired interests in most of the major US aircraft and aero accessories companies and the emergent airlines of the early thirties including well-known names like Douglas, Curtiss, Sperry Gyroscope, Ford Instrument, Eastern Airlines and Trans-Western Airlines. Eventually General Motors acquired an interest in North American Aviation and a subsequent re-organisation saw the name given to a new manufacturing concern to be headed by James H. Kindelberger, formerly a top

NIGHT AND DAY
Work on the NA-73X rarely stopped. Static testing was a slow and exacting business. This one was to test the wing to fuselage structural joint; quite simply, to see how much load it takes to pull the wing off. Hundreds of lead weights were used to obtain the answer.

CRASHED AND CRUMPLED

Test pilot Paul Balfour attempted a wheels-down landing when the engine of NA-73X stopped while flying 250 feet over Mines Field (now Los Angeles International Airport). He overshot the airfield boundary and put the prototype down in a cultivated field with this sad result. Luckily there was no fire, for Balfour was trapped in the cockpit and could not be released until rescuers had dug away soil. The farm shacks have long since given way to a more palatial structure, for the spot where the first Mustang came to grief is now covered by the International Hotel. Of interest are what appear to be gun ports in the wings but were, in fact, merely painted locations.

engineering executive with Douglas. New premises were established at Inglewood, near Los Angeles, and key personnel drawn from manufacturers within the old group, chiefly General Aviation Manufacturing Corporation, a company formerly building Fokker designs at Baltimore, Maryland. Kindelberger was an outstanding engineer (he had six years with Glenn Martin prior to his appointment with Douglas) and an astute business man, added to which his down-to-earth manner made a favourable impression on those with whom he dealt.

On 1st September 1939 the Nazis invaded Poland and two days later Britain and France honoured their guarantees to the Poles and declared war on Germany. The United States immediately enforced an arms embargo but there was no doubt that the President and the majority in Senate and Congress were not in favour of this act. Moves were quickly afoot to remedy the situation and two months later a Bill was passed permitting foreign powers to purchase arms for cash and carry them away in their own vessels. Within a matter of days the British and French were back

shopping in earnest for the complete range of military aircraft and equipment. By April 1940 over 10,000 aircraft were on order necessitating a vast expansion of the American aero industry. With the collapse of France the British took over the French contracts and continued to place new orders, and in some cases financing manufacturing facilities as well.

A Purchasing Board* under Sir Henry Self, a distinguished Civil Servant, operated from offices off New York's Wall Street and the staff included technicians and a test pilot. By the spring of 1940 the Board had a good knowledge of the vices and virtues of most current American combat aircraft. Construction was generally of a very high standard, but performance was often inadequate and military equipment insufficient or unsuitable to meet the standards expected by the RAF. Nowhere were the comparative deficiencies more marked than in the case of fighters—or pursuits, in American terminology of the time. The best of the single-seat

* Footnote: Officially the British Purchasing Commission.

10

fighters available to the Board was a Curtiss type entering Army Air Corps service as the P-40. This aircraft was fairly manoeuvrable and had a top speed of around 340mph between 12,000 and 15,000 feet, but the limitations of its Allison liquid-cooled engine, which had no super-charging, gave it a very poor showing above 15,000 ft. Large orders were placed for successive models of this fighter and Curtiss had contracts for some 1,740 from the British and French by the spring of 1940, in addition to those for the Army Air Corps.

As it would be several months before deliveries could be effected the Purchasing Board approached another manufacturer with a view to establishing a second source of production. At this juncture 'Dutch' Kindelberger offered the Purchasing Board North American's new twin-engine bomb-er design (subsequently developed as the Mitchell) and it was at this time that North American were invited to undertake the licence manufacture of the latest model Curtiss fighter. This proposal did not really appeal to Kindelberger although he

indicated a tentative interest. Later, in dis-cussing the matter with his associates at Inglewood, Kindelberger entertained the idea that North American could offer a fighter of their own design. This was prompted partly through difficulties en-visaged in adapting the Curtiss to their production methods and not least pride in their ability to produce a superior fighter. Time was the overriding consideration; how long would the British wait? Kindel-berger went back to see Sir Henry Self and put the proposal to him: North American would design a single-seat fighter around the same Allison engine used by the Curtiss and obtain a superior performance through an extremely low-drag airframe. The Com-pany would design the aircraft for mass production techniques to facilitate rapid manufacture.

Sir Henry, having dealt previously with Kindelberger on the Harvard contract, had respect for the man and his Company, both he and his advisers were sufficiently im-pressed to give the go-ahead for a pre-liminary design study. In view of North American's inexperience in the field of

NUMBER ONE
Top: The first production Mustang, AG345, photo-graphed in its original finish, April 1941. This aircraft served as a proto-type and remained with North American although later painted in RAF camouflage and colours.
NUMBER TEN
Above: The fourth and tenth Mustang Is were purchased for test by the USAAF as XP-51s. The latter, Army serial 41–39, formerly AG354, has radio and armament installed and also has the extended carburettor air intake found necessary after tests with AG345.

11

fighter design—the nearest they had come was adding a more powerful engine and a few machine guns to a single-seat version of the Harvard type trainer—and the possible production and development pitfalls, this decision showed a remarkable degree of confidence. It was not misplaced and was to prove almost momentous.

A telegram alerting the design engineers at Inglewood was sent on Saturday 24th April and Chief Engineer Raymond Rice put his team to work. Kindelberger flew back to California leaving his number two, John Atwood, behind in New York to handle negotiations. Working through the night the design staff had the general arrangement drawings and a preliminary weight study ready for Kindelberger's ap-

proval by 10 the following morning. Kindelberger liked what he saw, drawings of a beautifully sleek, low-winged monoplane where every effort had been made to keep drag factors to a minimum. There was nothing fancy about the design: it had a very functional appearance. The basic drawings were made by Edgar Schmued, North American's chief designer, who had started his career in aeronautics in his native Bavaria.

The plans and data were airmailed to Atwood in New York who presented them to the Purchasing Board. Sir Henry Self's service and technical advisers, Air Vice-Marshal G. B. A. Baker and H. C. B. Thomas were greatly impressed and gave Atwood the order to proceed. Negotiations

continued on detailed specification and price with the Board eventually accepting $50,000 as the cost per unit ex-factory. These meetings culminated in an order, dated 29th May 1940, for 320 of the new fighter which was identified by the Company designation NA-73.

There were certain provisos in the contract. Not only must the aircraft meet the specification but the prototype was to be ready in four months—the time it would have taken to prepare for production of the Curtiss at Inglewood. This was a formidable target which Kindelberger and Atwood seemed confident they could meet and assured the Purchasing Board. Nevertheless, the practical problems were immense and how they were overcome is a

story of extraordinary enterprise and skill.

Using the same Allison power plant as the Curtiss, similar armament and war equipment, yet achieving a vastly superior performance from aircraft of similar size could only be effected by superior streamlining and weight savings. The North American design team began by seeking to minimise drag wherever possible. The nose of the aircraft featured a close fitting and beautifully streamlined engine cowling with only the carburettor air intake breaking its lines. The fuselage cross section area aft of the engine was reduced to the minimum without unduly restricting vision from the cockpit, this was achieved by 'sinking' the transparent canopy well into the fuselage. The aerodynamic bugbear of

NUMBER TWO
AG346, the first Mustang in British colours, with war equipment, and the first despatched to the UK. No better proof of the soundness of basic Mustang design existed than this first of the many. More than three years after this photograph was taken she was still very much at war. On 20th August 1944 AG346 was hit by flak north east of Gace, France, and reported 'Not Yet Returned' with pilot F/Lt D. Clark. But she turned up safely and was back in action within a few days.

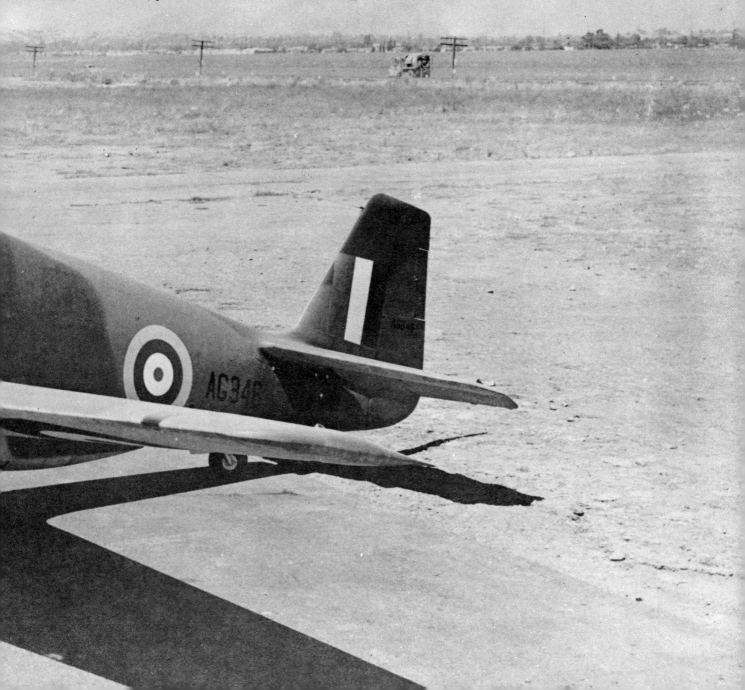

any aircraft incorporating a liquid-cooled engine was the placing of the large radiator necessary to provide adequate cooling of the glycol mixture. With the NA-73 Schmued and aerodynamist Edward Horkey chose to place this as far to the rear of the aircraft as practicable, in order to preserve the nose streamlining and delay the drag factor. It was further proposed to attempt a reduction of radiator frontal area by employing aerodynamic principles in the design of the entry ducting. Finally, a bold decision was made to give the aircraft a wing employing the so-called laminar flow airfoil, a comparatively untried section developed by the US National Advisory Committee for Aeronautics.

The descriptive name for the airfoil comes from its feature of keeping the layers of air passing across the wing in even though compressed layers. The laminar flow wing attained its maximum thickness farther back along the chord than airfoils hitherto used in fighter wing designs, this resulting in smooth flow over the curvature of the wing for a greater distance and consequently delaying the appearance of drag inducing eddies. While affording drag reductions and good lift qualities in all but low speed ranges, early experiments had shown it more sensitive to surface irregularities such as indentations or even scratches. A quarter-size wing of laminated mahogany, finished to .001-inch tolerances was made and tested in the wind tunnel at the California Institute of Technology. The wing proved to have the lowest drag coefficient of any so far tested in the USA, but there was evidence of bad stall characteristics. Faced with this problem it seemed that a wing with orthodox airfoil might have to be substituted, a possibility already allowed for but estimated to require an extra month to design and test. After modifying the laminar design, a further

wind tunnel test, run a week later, proved equally disappointing. However, as turbulence at the wing tips suggested that the model was too large for the wind tunnel, arrangements were made to conduct a test in the largest tunnel available, that at Seattle, Washington. Here the design team were relieved to discover that the wing tip turbulence had abated.

Another novel feature of the NA-73 was the cantilever box beam structure to marry the complete engine installation to the fuselage. This also acted as a securing base for the cowling, facilitating easy removal for inspection.

Time hung inexorably over this project like the proverbial sword of Damocles, and the design team were ever conscious of clock and calendar. While work proceeded with undeniable haste, it was characterised by exceptional care and competent management. Every mathematical and aerodynamic computation had to be absolutely accurate. Kindelberger and Atwood had clear ideas on the mass production aspects and from the outset planned that the NA-73 should be designed for this technique. Moreover, as each component was designed, a wooden mock-up was constructed to aid production plans and show if the items of equipment to be installed in the aircraft could be fitted in the designated location satisfactorily. In this way snags were revealed at the planning stages permitting solutions before application to the actual airframe.

Work on the prototype went ahead at an accelerating pace. In contrast to contemporary European designs the NA-73 employed a great many castings; some, which had to be contracted out to specialist manufacturers, were watched over by North American staff who were ready to carry off a part the moment it was completed. Engineers worked on plans and the prototype for long hours, sometimes through the night. The urgency to meet the target date was imbued on everyone's mind. Some 2,800 design drawings were involved with the prototype. Difficulties were few, and by early August it appeared as if the NA-73X (X designated the prototype) would be completed in advance of the target date. The only major problem was that the engine—common to the US Army's Lockheed P-38, Bell P-39 and Curtiss P-40 fighters, and in great demand—was not forthcoming from Allisons. In consequence, a good deal of 'red tape' had to be surmounted before the Army would release an engine—and the spinners of red tape were unaccustomed to urgency.

By early August the airframe was practically complete and to mark the hundredth day since the order was received, the NA-73X airframe was given a ceremonial roll-out on makeshift wheel equipment. Not until early October was the Allison delivered, when it was fitted within a day and taxiing trials began almost immediately. Vance Breese, a distinguished test pilot, made the first NA-73X flight on 26th October, 1940. No difficulties were encountered and there was understandable jubilation from the North American team, for when contemporary designs were taking two to three years from the contracted date to first flight, North American's feat can be literally considered fantastic. In the light of the subsequent acclaim for the design, the feat is all the more remarkable.

It would be wrong to suggest the flights of NA-73X did not indicate some shortcomings, although only one proved really troublesome and this had not been entirely unexpected. The first few flights revealed a tendency for the Allison to overheat indicating that the cooling had to be improved. However, before much work could be done disaster struck; on its fifth flight the engine cut out (due to a fuel switching error) and in an attempted deadstick wheels down landing in a cultivated field the machine ended up on its back, sustaining major damage.

Enough hours had been achieved with NA-73X for the makers and the British Purchasing Commission to have every confidence that the design was sound and superior to other US built fighter types. Even before the prototype's first flight, while it still waited engineless in Inglewood hangar No. 1 a further production order for 300 aircraft was made. Kindelberger hastened work on the production line; there was no slackening of effort even though the total contracts for 620 machines could give North American steady work for nearly three years.

The first production aircraft, British serial number AG345, was completed on 16th April 1941 and took to the air during the last week of that month. Exactly one year had passed since 'Dutch' Kindelberger had obtained Sir Henry Self's go ahead on the preliminary design!

In the late 1930s radio programmes on both sides of the Atlantic were playing a catchy song that ran: "Saddle your blues to a wild mustang and gallop your troubles away, away." It is said that someone in the British Air Council section assigned the task of finding acceptable names for wartime aircraft recalled this jingle, and suggested Mustang for the NA-73. The name had the required American flavour plus a touch of aggressiveness which was desirable for a fighter type. Yet the first Mustangs were far from wild, earning a reputation for docility from the men who went to war in them.

Origin of the Mustang

John Leland Atwood

North American Aviation's chief negotiator with the British Purchasing Commission for aircraft orders was the company's Vice-President "Lee" Atwood. An astute businessman, he became President of the company in 1948 and later of North American Rockwell, holding office until his retirement in 1970. The following is his personal account of the initial moves that led to the design and production of the Mustang.

At the outbreak of the war in 1939 North American Aviation was in production of the Harvard trainer for the British and French governments and had made a very good record for quality aircraft and prompt delivery. The company had also built two prototype medium bombers, the NA-21 and the NA-40, and had received its first production order for the B-25 "Mitchell" bomber.

I had been Vice President and Chief Engineer, but about this time, Mr. Kindelberger, who was President and General Manager, asked me to become Vice President and Assistant General Manager. At about the same time, J. Stanley Smithson moved from Chief Project Engineer to Vice President— Manufacturing and Production, and Raymond H. Rice moved from Assistant Chief Engineer to Chief Engineer.

In the late fall of 1939, someone in the British Purchasing Commission had suggested to Mr. Kindelberger that North American Aviation consider establishing a production line for the Curtiss P-40 to augment production for this model. This request was not put with any urgency, and this proposal was not seriously considered at that time.

However, I had been thinking about the possibility of designing a fighter at North American and had, at various times, examined the P-40. It seemed apparent to me that a considerably better design could be developed, and I evolved a design concept which involved placing the coolant radiators back of the wing and designed a ducting system to recover some of the cooling energy in an efficient manner. This principle had been developed to some extent in literature, both in the United States (NACA) and in England as the "Meredith effect." It involved discharging the heated air under as much pressure as was possible in a rear facing jet as in the yet-to-be-developed ram-jet engine. Thus, the cooling drag could be reduced to very little or even nothing at all in theory. The P-40 had the radiators, both engine heat rejection and oil coolers, suspended under the engine, giving a poor aerodynamic entry, and no effort was made to restore the momentum of the cooling air, the discharge merely leaking out through openings in the cowling at the firewall.

However, as far as I know, no drawings of this new concept were made at that time, and I did not authorize any design work until considerably later.

In January, 1940, the British had renewed their suggestion that North American build some P-40s, and at this time, with the concurrence of Mr. Kindelberger, I approached the British Purchasing Commission which was then headed by Sir Henry Self, with the idea that North American could design and build a fighter plane superior to the P-40 in a reasonably short time. My principal contacts subsequently were Colonel William Cave and Air Commodore Baker, who assisted Sir Henry Self in his mission. This suggestion was taken under consideration, and I was called upon to confer with Colonel Cave and Air Commodore Baker from time to time on the company's background, our technical capabilities, further questions as to the configuration we proposed, etc.

I made several trips to New York from January to April and stayed at the Essex House most of the time. The British offices were located at 15 Broad Street. I received some assistance from the General

Motors offices at 1775 Broadway, not far from the Essex House. Also, I was assisted from time to time by R. L. Burla of the North American Aviation staff and L. R. Taylor, then based in Washington, D.C. for the company. A. T. Burton who had been stationed in England for the Harvard program also assisted. The Chadbourne law firm gave me legal assistance, mainly through Ralph Ray, a partner in the firm.

I made it clear that we had no dseign, but that if authorized to proceed, we would design and build the aircraft in accordance with the representations I had made to the British Purchasing Commision. These conversations went on until about the last week in March or the first week in April, when apparently affirmative recommendations were made to Sir Henry Self.

At that time he called me in and discussed the project and asked me for a definite proposal. He made a reservation, however, and took note of the fact that we had not ever designed an actual fighter plane. He asked me if I thought I could get copies of the wind tunnel tests and flight tests of the P-40 airplane. He said if I could, it would increase their confidence in our ability to move forward in a timely way. I told him I would try, and that night I took the train to Buffalo where I called upon Mr. Burdett Wright who was General Manager of the Curtiss Division at Buffalo. After negotiating with him for most of a day, I arranged to purchase copies of the wind tunnel tests and the flight test report for the sum of $56,000 which would cover the out-of-pocket expenses and some proportion of the cost of the tests.

I went back to New York and indicated to Sir Henry that I had been able to secure the data and presented him with a draft of a letter contract which called for the production of 320 NA-73 aircraft equipped with an Allison engine and certain armaments to be furnished by the British, and an airframe to be designed and built by North American Aviation—the total cost to the British Government excluding engine, armaments, etc., was not to exceed $40,000 per airplane.

Although some technical work was by then being done in Los Angeles, we had not at this time presented the British Purchasing Commission with drawings or specifications of any kind except for free-hand sketches I had used to demonstrate the concept in informal conversations, and the letter contract was the sole document available. Sir Henry Self executed this document, after having it edited by his legal staff, and with this instrument the Mustang project got underway.

I should add one point—which is that the original concept did not include the laminar flow wing, which was eventually incorporated. This wing design came from the aerodynamics department of the North American Aviation engineering group headed by L. L. Waite, and the concept was originated by Edward Horkey who was one of the aerodynamic specialists. His work was based on very recent developments of the NACA (National Advisory Committee for Aeronautics, which later became NASA — National Aeronautics and Space Administration).

The engineering department was then headed by Raymond Rice, who had recently succeeded me as Chief Engineer, and Edgar Schmued was Assistant Chief Engineer and chief of the preliminary design group. The drawings were prepared under his general supervision and that of Raymond Rice and other senior personnel in the engineering department.

The total production of the Mustang, including the A-36 and the P-51 through the P-51D, was approximately 15,000 aircraft, all built at Los Angeles and Dallas, Texas. Thousands of people, including many fine engineers, contributed to the development and perfection of this aircraft, and the fact that engineering improvement never ceased is one of the principal factors in its overall success.

The Downstairs Maid

On a grey day in October 1941 a Focke-Wulf Condor of a Luftwaffe anti-shipping unit encountered an Atlantic convoy bound for Britain. The vessel selected for an attack survived little damaged and proceeded to Liverpool, docking on the 24th. Among her cargo was a large wooden crate containing AG346, the second production Mustang and first example to reach the United Kingdom. The crate was taken to nearby Speke aerodrome where the machine was unpacked and carefully prepared for flying. Tests followed and pilots soon confirmed the favourable flight characteristics that had been reported from California.

A profusion of crated Mustangs began to arrive at Liverpool during following weeks as production at Inglewood got into stride. The Atlantic crossing was ex-tremely hazardous at the time with German submarines taking a heavy toll of British shipping, including one of the early shipments of Mustangs. All told, 25 Mustangs were lost at sea in transit, most of these during 1942.

Deliveries of the first Mustangs to Britain had been delayed for small modifications due to snags that were not highlighted until the first production aircraft was under flight test. Air starvation of the carburettor in some speed ranges necessitated slight enlargement of the intake duct, and extending it forward to the edge of the engine cowling. Alterations were also made to the radiator housing scoop, the bottom edge being lowered an inch to obtain a non-turbulent air flow for adequate cooling.

Flight tests in Britain showed that war

equipped and loaded, the Mustang I could consistently attain a top speed of 375mph at 15,000 feet; 35mph faster than the RAF's standard low/medium altitude fighter of the day, the Spitfire V. The Mustang was heavier than the Spitfire V— around 8,6000lb loaded as against 6,900lb —and in consequence did not climb so quickly, taking 11 minutes to reach 20,000 feet to the Spitfire's 7 minutes. Above 15,000 feet the performance of the Mustang fell away due to lack of any supercharging on the Allison.

Two Mustangs from an early consignment were delivered to the Air Fighting Development Unit at Duxford, south of Cambridge, for the evaluation of its combat worthiness. During February they were pitted against the RAF Spitfires and other types in comparison tests from which the

Mustang emerged with a great deal of credit and little in default. The report rated the aircraft with a high standard of manufacture with good servicing facilities. The cockpit layout was excellent with throttle controls and other major levers and switches well placed for operation by the pilot's left hand while the right was free to hold the 'stick'. Visibility from the cockpit was better than that from the Spitfire, although the low roof line meant that a tall pilot would find his legs rather cramped with the seat in its bottom position. The low slung and rear positioned radiator received a substantial blast from the propeller; while this aided cooling on the ground, on a loose surface the propeller tended to blast up small stones and other objects into the scoop with the risk of damage to the core. While this was not applicable on airfields with concrete runways and dispersal points, the grass fields from which the Mustang would be likely to operate could present a hazard.

In flight the aircraft was stable and smooth to control. It built up very high speeds in a dive with recovery effected fairly easily. A four-hour endurance was about double that of the Spitfire or other contemporary single-engined fighters. Its critical altitude was reached at some 12,000 feet, above which performance gradually fell off until at 25,000 feet the reduction in power was so appreciable that the aircraft

DEBUT AT BLEAK SPEKE Above/Left: The fifth Mustang I, AG349, was first of its kind shown to the press and officialdom in the United Kingdom. Two days before the Japanese struck at Pearl Harbor this aircraft was displayed with a Curtis Kittyhawk in front of the airport building at Speke as the latest acquisitions from the US aviation industry. Armament details of the Mustang were still secret at this date and the censor required that any sign of guns should be painted out on these photographs. AG349 went to Farnborough for comparison trials with other fighter types before seeing service with Canadian 430 Squadron.

BRAND NEW 'WORKS'
Below/Below right: Early arrivals were assembled at Speke where each Mustang arrived in a single wooden crate measuring 9ft × 10ft × 35ft. The neat layout of instruments and controls was a notable feature but unpopular was the separate slab of armoured glass placed between the gun sight and the moulded Lucite (Perspex) windshield. Misting was a frequent problem and the hot air demister was of little help. Bullet-proof glass was incorporated in the wind-shield on Mustang Is of the second batch ordered. The two 0.50 inch calibre machine guns, synchronised to fire through the propeller arc, were buried beneath the Allison with actuating mechanism and storage for 400 rounds of ammunition. The barrels projected through blast tubes.

became quite unwieldy to control. In comparison tests the Mustang proved faster than the Spitfire VB in level flight up to 20,000 feet, and it could frequently turn with the Spitfire at these lower altitudes by the prudent use of flaps. Against the Messerschmitt Bf 109E the Mustang also showed superior manoeuvrability and speed at low altitudes, but this model of the German fighter was no longer in front line service.

The conclusions endorsed previous find-ings that the Mustang I was—to use their pilots' vernacular—not suited to work 'up-stairs'. The aircraft was ideally fitted for the lower realms of air combat, indeed, it was to become very much a 'downstairs maid'.

A decision on the employment of the Mustang had not been made prior to its testing in the United Kingdom. Handling and performance reports from RAF test pilots in the USA had noted the limitations that the Allison imposed on the aircraft,

limitations that were already evident from trials with the other Allison-powered types also supplied to Britain. With the crisis of 1940 past, and home production of fighter types gathering momentum, the RAF chose to concentrate on improved Spitfire models for the interceptor role where good high altitude performance was imperative. The possibility of maintenance and supply problems with an imported type, through shipping losses, was another factor influencing Fighter Command's standardisation on indigenous fighters. While the Mustang offered advantages in range and dive performance, deficiencies at high altitude made it unacceptable. Rejected by Fighter Command the Mustang was gladly accepted by Army Co-operation Command, where a really fast and manoeuvrable aircraft was needed for the fighter-reconnaissance concept then being developed.

Army Co-operation Command was established in December 1940 to "organise, experiment and train in all forms of land-air co-operation". It was the direct outcome of the disastrous experiences in the spring battles in France when the old concept of air support for the Army proved hopelessly inadequate. Slow reconnaissance types like the Lysander were found too vulnerable to both enemy ground and air opposition. In their place the RAF came to use fast, heavily armed, fighter air-

craft able to subdue enemy ground fire with return fire, hold their own against interceptors, and bring back observed or photographic intelligence with speed. The Tomahawk used initially by the new Command suffered a high rate of unserviceability; with the advent of the Mustang these could be retired. The plan was to convert existing squadrons flying Lysanders and Tomahawks and, during 1942, to form six new units towards an ultimate force of 18 Mustang squadrons. In the event, there was never more than 16 at any one time.

The first squadron to receive a Mustang was No. 26 which collected one from Speke late in January and flew it down to Gatwick, then a grass field in the Surrey hills. In March Mustangs began to appear in some numbers at many of the small Army Co-operation airfields dotted about the length of Britain—Sawbridgeworth in Hertfordshire, Clifton and Doncaster in Yorkshire and Bottisham and Snailwell in Cambridgeshire being among the first. By May, half a dozen squadrons had received Mustangs, although most were only partly equipped and none were operational.

The primary function of Army Co-operation Command was, as the name implies, supporting Army operations. In 1942 ground forces in the United Kingdom training for forthcoming campaigns involved Mustang units in countless exer-

COME ON, 'ARRY— WHERE THE 'ELL ARE YOU?
Above/Above left: Fitters put their weight on a jig to right a wing section as a crane lifts. The Mustang was designed so that major components could be easily taken apart for shipping. When the wing was positioned correctly and the undercarriage extended and locked down, the fuselage was lifted from the floor of the shipping crate and lowered carefully on to it. This machine, AG585, spent its life with 41 OTU at Hawarden—not far from the assembly field at Speke—where many RAF Mustang pilots learned to handle the type.

Close-up in the Clover

On sunny 24th July 1942, No. 2 Squadron put its Mustangs through their paces for the benefit of 50 press representatives visiting Sawbridgeworth. The cameramen took these detailed pictures.

Top left: The flaps that could be inched down to make very tight turns.

Upper left: Undercarriage detail. Wheel cover doors closed to improve air flow after leg was extended.

Lower left: Variable discharge scoop for air passing through the radiator. Hole in letter B is for locating a hoist or tying down aircraft.

Bottom left: Leading edge landing light and pitot tube on starboard wing.

Top centre: Cockpit area. F24 camera was situated in aperture aft of pilot's seat. It used a 5in × 5in film of 125 or 250 exposures. Pilot is P/O W. R. Butt.

Above: Nose and propeller detail. Early Mustang Is did not have provision for gun camera in the nose compartment.

Left: Daisy Cutting: A few feet above the airfield AG623, XV:W, gives a demonstration run, while AG456, XV:B weaves above. These are the two aircraft featured in detail on the previous page.

cises to develop air-ground co-operation. The seemingly unhurried introduction of the Mustang I to combat operations was because there was no immediate combat requirement to fulfil. While the Mustang could not play its assigned role in full until the Army went to war, the Command planned to test its potential in missions to the hostile side of the English Channel.

The Mustang squadron had exercised in tactical reconnaissance, observation and photography of 'enemy' forces in and behind the battle area. For this work the Mustangs had an F24 camera installed behind the pilot's seat, above the radios, sited to 'shoot' obliquely through a small aperture in the glazing. Operating in pairs, at low altitudes, the leader concentrating on taking reconnaissance photos while his 'No. 2' or 'Weaver' kept watch for enemy interceptors. With reconnaissance the object, pilots were trained not to engage enemy aircraft in combat unless attacked— and this applied when Army Co-operation squadrons did eventually fly sorties against a real enemy. Their introduction came on 10th May when a single Mustang, AG418, piloted by F/O G. N. Dawson of 26 Squadron took off from Gatwick at 0450 hours for an offensive reconnaissance of the Berck-sur-Mer area on the French coast. After crossing the coast the Mustang swept low over Berck airfield where the pilot observed vehicles and packing cases. He fired at two hangars in the south-east corner and then made off, an unhealthy quantity of light anti-aircraft shells and machine gun bullets in his wake. A goods train seen at La Fesnesie received a burst of fire as the Mustang made good its escape, arriving safely back at Gatwick an hour and forty minutes after its departure.

Thereafter Mustangs of 26 Squadron made fairly regular forays into hostile territory and inevitably the time came when one did not return. This first Mustang lost in action was AG415, piloted by P/O H. Taylor, on 14th July. The aircraft was thought to have struck a barge it was strafing near Le Touquet.

On 19th August the so-called 'reconnaissance in force' was carried out at Dieppe, when in an amphibious operation Army formations were put ashore and later withdrawn. Mustangs of Army Co-

operation Command provided continual photographic and observed intelligence of the situation at Dieppe and the vicinity throughout the day flying, in all, 72 sorties. Four squadrons were involved, the already operational 26 and 239 Squadrons, plus 400 and 414 Canadian Squadrons making their combat debut. The Mustangs suffered severely at the hands of the Luftwaffe and German flak gunners, nine being lost, two others damaged beyond repair, and several with minor damage. No. 414 Squadron's baptism of fire resulted in the first known claim of an enemy aircraft destroyed by a Mustang.

While 'Popular'* sorties continued to be the principal type of Mustang operation during the summer and autumn of 1942, the type was also detached to fly shipping reconnaissance off the Dutch coast in the hope of identifying enemy vessels for attack by fighter-bombers. There was revived interest by Fighter Command in the Mustang's low altitude fighter potential when some were requested for the interception of wave-hopping FW 190s making hit and run raids on south coast towns.

* Code name for low altitude photographic reconnaissance operation over enemy coastal regions, taking advantage of cloud cover.

TWO FOR A FIRST
Left/Above: AL995,XV:S and AM112,XV:X, piloted by Sqn Ldr A. E. Houseman and F/Lt G. Kenning respectively, carried out 2 Squadron's first Mustang operation, a 'Popular' on 14th November 1942, with the approaches to a Dutch coastal radar station as the objective. AL995—here seen parked for radiator repair— endured a great many operations with various squadrons to the end of hostilities. AM112, George Kenning's personal aircraft, was one of 2 Squadron's longest serving Mustangs. The nationally known Kenning car empire was George Kenning's vocation in post-war years.

THREE FOR A FLAP

Above: Just a little allows Sqn Ldr E. M. Goodale's AM148 to stay with the photographer's aircraft. A few days after this picture was taken Mike Goodale took AM148,RM:G on its first and only combat sortie with 26 Sqn., the Dieppe operation of 19th August 1942. On return to Gatwick the Mustang over-ran the runway and hit an obstruction, all due to brake failure caused by an enemy bullet severing a hydraulic connection. AM148 was withdrawn for repair and later, in June 1943, it was sent to Rolls-Royce at Hucknall to be fitted with a Griffon engine. This project was abandoned at an early stage and AM148 went to the scrap heap.

Right: Caught in partial silhouette a Mustang I of No. 4 Squadron uses 40 degrees to execute a sharp turn. Hydraulically actuated, the flaps took between 4 and 6 seconds to traverse the full 50 degrees.

Right: Full down for landing. AG602 of 613 Squadron making an approach at York. On 7th December 1942, a few weeks after this photograph was taken, this aircraft failed to return from a Rhubarb. Individual Army Co-operation Command squadrons were attached to specific Army formations and often carried the latter's approved insignia. The panda head painted on the noses of 613 Sqn. Mustangs was that of the 9th Armoured Division.

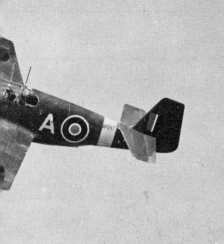

LONG STAYER

Left: The average life of an Allison Mustang was about a year. AL247 was one of a small number that survived in squadron service until the end of hostilities. A late production Mark I, she was taken on charge by 4 Squadron in October 1942. For the early part of her service with this squadron she was the CO's personal kite—she wears a Wing Commander's pennant in this picture—and took part in many Rhubarb and Popular operations. W/C 'Mac' MacDonald was lost while flying another Mustang (see text). After a spell with 309 Squadron this Mustang went to 26 Squadron in November 1944 and was used for V-2 launch-site spotting flights. Finally, she was Struck off Charge on 18th June 1945.

PRACTISING THE ART

Below: With low cloud enveloping the hilltops, two Mustangs of 63 Squadron speed along at 300 mph seventy feet above farm lands at Tranent, East Lothian, 5th April 1943. As if flight at such speed and altitude was not task enough, a pilot was required to map-read, report observed intelligence to his HQ, record this and messages received on a pad strapped to his knee, and keep a sharp lookout for enemy interceptors. "It kept you busy", was typical pilot's understatement of the job.

ONE THAT DIDN'T
Right/Far right: No 241 Squadron never had a chance to take its brand new Mustangs to war for in November 1942, in company with two other Army Co-operation Command squadrons it was despatched —less aircraft—to the new North African front to fly Hurricanes. In the previous August, while stationed at Ayr, 241's CO, Wing Commander J. L. Barker and four of his pilots (L. to R., F/Lt O. D. B. Coe, P/O J. W. S. Smith, F/Lt K. Plumtree and P/O J. A. Hamlet) posed for this photograph with the squadron mascot. The Mustang, AG645, carries F/Lt Plumtree's personal motif. Apart from the British roundels, authorised markings on squadron service Mustangs at this date were the Sky (duck-egg blue) squadron identification code letters, propeller spinner and rear fuselage band distinguishing it as a 'friendly fighter type'. Additionally, the Mustang had a narrow yellow band painted round each wing, as a special recognition marking because of the widely held belief that any fighter with square wing tips was an Me 109. However, this marking was discontinued early in 1943 as it proved to be of little practical value. At the same time the two letters of the squadron code were removed.

ONE THAT DID
Bottom right: The Mustangs of 241 Squadron were taken over in November 1942 by 168 Squadron which saw plenty of action in them during the following months. No. 168 was one of five RAF reconnaissance Mustang squadrons to operate on the Continent after D-day. In this photograph, taken at Odiham in February 1943, the sleek lines of the Mustangs contrast with blunt profile of the 'Lizzie', the Westland Lysander, original workhorse of Army Co-operation Command. Mustang AG512 (marked RZ:A) was still serving with 168 Sqn when it finally relinquished the type in late September 1944.

Others were detailed for special escorts of aircraft from Coastal and Bomber Commands where no other RAF single-engined fighter had the necessary range.

By October, however, the operational Mustang force had grown to over 200 aircraft, more than meeting the current demand for tactical reconnaissance, so alternative operations were introduced and, like the Populars, they were performed under the control of Fighter Command. These were Rhubarbs, daylight intrusions to seek and attack specified types of target with machine-gun fire undertaken only when low cloud conditions prevailed. As Rhubarbs would normally involve up to four aircraft which would be at a defensive disadvantage if attacked by enemy fighters at low altitude, these operations were never flown if the weather was better than 7/10ths cloud at 1,500 feet. In other words, these were bad weather operations and, commencing in mid-October 1942, they were conducted regularly whenever conditions were favourable until the spring of 1944. The targets were enemy aircraft and airfields, military installations and enemy rail, road and water borne transportation; the area of activity stretched from the Brest peninsula to the north German coast. On one of their first Rhubarbs Mustangs penetrated to the Dortmund-Ems Canal,

the first occasion single-engine fighter aircraft flying from Britain had entered German air space. An extension of these activities was the introduction, early in 1943, of Ranger missions with similar objectives but the participants operated on a freelance basis. Only the Mustang had the range for such sorties, its radius of action being taken as 300 miles in planning these operations, twice the distance specified for Spitfires, Hurricanes and Typhoons. Even with long range drop-tanks the Spitfires and Hurricanes were only able to reach 210 miles from base.

The flight out would be made at an average of 230mph and speed increased to 300mph over hostile territory. Losses were generally light as the Mustang pilots usually had the element of surprise. Nevertheless, low altitude ground attack was highly dangerous for, if an aircraft was badly hit, there was usually insufficient height for a pilot to safely take to his parachute. Some men were lost in unusual circumstances. The popular, fast-talking CO of No. 4 Squadron, Wing Commander G. E. 'Mac' Macdonald, met his death on a Rhubarb over Holland on 28th April 1943 when a munitions barge he shot up on a canal near Hasselt exploded just as his aircraft passed overhead. There was always the risk of flying into a ground obstruction.

A tragedy of this nature occurred on 3rd May 1943 when a four-plane flight from 2 Squadron was returning from strafing rail targets in the Rennes area. Nearing the Dorset coast the low-flying aircraft suddenly encountered sea fog. The leader radioed the others to climb but unfortunately before they had escaped the mists the flight made landfall at St. Albans Head, a 150 feet high cliff, where the three others flew into it, killing the pilots.

Squadrons took turns in the offensive effort against enemy ground targets in between the continuing programme of exercises with the army. Even so, some squadrons were particularly successful, notably Nos. 268 and 613 and the two Canadian Nos. 400 and 414; these four accounting for almost all the 30-odd enemy fighters brought down by Allison-engined RAF Mustangs. Pilots of 400 Squadron had destroyed or badly damaged more than a hundred locomotives in their first six months of Rhubarb and Ranger missions, and they went on to claim a dozen enemy aircraft in the air within a year. Commencing in June 1943 the squadron also did occasional night intruder operations by lone Mustangs, and on consecutive nights in August shot down enemy night fighters over their French bases.

Canada's Pride

Among the most distinguished Mustang units were two squadrons of the Royal Canadian Air Force No 400 (City of Toronto) and No 414 (Sarnia Imperials) that went to war at Dieppe and were rarely away from the action from then on. Mustang history was made by pilots of these units.

FIRST KILL

Above: Flying Officer Hollis H. Hills, 414 Squadron, had the distinction of being credited with the first enemy aircraft shot down by a Mustang. Interestingly, he was an American volunteer in the RCAF and hailed from Los Angeles near the Mustang's birthplace. The action occurred during the Dieppe operation when Hills was flying AG470 and acting as a Weaver.

On his second sortie (1025-1140 hrs) the radio failed and he was unable to warn his Flight Commander when three FW 190s attacked. He therefore engaged the enemy himself and shot one down. The Flight Commander was F/Lt F. E. Clarke who gave this version of the incident: "F/O Hills and I took off to carry out a reconnaissance of the Dieppe area. F/O Hills was flying cover for me. We crossed the coast at St Auburn sur Mer and I picked up the road which was my task and had followed it in behind Dieppe. Then I was jumped by a Focke-Wulf 190 which shot my oil and glycol cooler away. I immediately turned tight left and three-quarters of the way round the turn I saw that my oil pressure was nil. My engine started to seize. I immediately straightened out, used my excess speed to gain height to about 800 feet and headed for the sea off Dieppe. Just before straightening out, on my port rear quarter I saw a FW 190 with grey smoke pouring from it heading towards a wood apparently out of control. In my opinion it was impossible for the pilot to do anything but pile up in the wood. This is definitely the aircraft which F/O Hills claims as destroyed."

Hollis Hills transferred to the US Navy and flew with a carrier fighter squadron for the remainder of the war.

A WING AND A PRAYER

Left/Top to bottom: Another incident at Dieppe showed what a Mustang could take and still keep flying. It involved Pilot Officer Charles H. Stover and AG601 and resulted from violent evasive action to escape the attentions of a FW 190. This is 'Smoky' Stover's account:

"I was a member of No 414 based at Croydon but for the Dieppe operation our squadron, along with RAF No 268, were moved to Gatwick the evening before because of the possibility of early morning fog and haze in the London area. As it happened this was the first venture into enemy territory by any member of our squadron with our comparatively new Mustangs and naturally all pilots had considerable apprehension about the whole exercise but everyone was very keen to have a 'go'.

"A considerable portion of my starboard wing and aileron suddenly 'went missing' after contact with a French telephone pole and I am firmly convinced that if it had not been for the considerable strength built into the aircraft my first sortie into France would also have been my last. The aircraft was reasonably controllable at maximum continuous cruise power with the aid of aileron trim of which fortunately there was some left on the starboard side. The aircraft developed an uncontrollable roll to the right when the airspeed dropped to 200 mph IAS

or thereabouts. I felt there was sufficient handling ability left to attempt a landing wheels down which I did on return to Gatwick. Touching down at 175/200 mph on the short strips, probably the longest in those days at Gatwick was 1,500 yds, made for an exciting landing and a necessary quick stop. I can remember being concerned about over-running into the 20 ft deep anti-tank ditch that surrounded the airport and on the first touch of brakes the aircraft went up on its nose and slid to a nice easy stop with the nose resting on one of the prop-blades still on the grass runway well short of the ditch."
Bottom photograph shows Charles Stover with pet 'Blackie' at Dunsfold in January 1944, when commanding 414.

HANK

Right: Another highly successful pilot in 400 Squadron was F/O Frank Hanton. By October 1943, when he was awarded the DFC, he had shot down one enemy aircraft, shared another, probably destroyed two and damaged one. The air victory was also the first obtained by a Mustang at night, when in brilliant moonlight on 14th August 1943, 'Hank' Hanton caught an Me 110 preparing to land at an airfield near Rennes.

LONG RANGE FIGHTER

Above left: The first maximum endurance sorties involving Mustangs were for the purpose of destroying enemy aircraft that harassed Allied shipping and air

operations in the Bay of Biscay. Early in June 1943 No 414 Squadron moved to Portreath, Cornwall, to undertake these duties. On the 6th F/O Rowan Hutchinson put up a remarkable show that was also something of a milestone in tactical performance for a single-engine, single-seat fighter. The squadron record detailed the operation as follows:

"Squadron was warned to provide four aircraft for a special escort task for the Navy for 1700 . . . (Red Section) made contact with the ship about 1730 and were relieved at 1910 by Blue Section (F/O R. T. Hutchinson in AM167 and F/O L. A. Dogerty in AP172). At about 2030 F/O Hutchinson heard his

Number 2 give a very brief warning that they were being attacked. He immediately took violent evasive action and saw F/O Dogerty's aircraft going into the sea at a steep angle with black smoke pouring from it. At the time of the attack our aircraft were flying at 50–75 feet. F/O Hutchinson was then attacked by each of the three enemy aircraft which he identified as FW 190s. Attacks continued for approximately 20 minutes during which time F/O Hutchinson got in two bursts but did not observe strikes. Enemy aircraft abandoned attacks and Blue 1 continued escorting the ship. During the combat the ship was not attacked. The ship then turned a reciprocal course and was escorted back to base. F/O Hutchinson did not leave the ship although he had almost exhausted his petrol and finally landed after a patrol of 4 hours with 17 gallons of petrol left."

BITSY

Above: F/Lt Duncan Grant of 400 Sqdn. had an un-surpassed score for RAF reconnaissance Mustang pilots; three aircraft destroyed and one 'probable'. He also put paid to 30 locomotives during strafing raids. 'Bitsy' Grant 'bought it' near Ault on 28th September 1943 when his hedge-hopping Mustang took a direct flak hit and crashed into trees.

MAPLELEAF STRONGHOLD

In the winter of 1942–43 the Canadian Mustang squadrons were established at newly constructed Dunsfold airfield in Surrey, under the command of W/C E. H. Moncrieff. A third squadron, No 430, began forming early in 1943 and by late summer there were between 50 and 60 Mustangs on the field. The mud surrounding the dispersal points in early spring had been covered with a lush growth of grass by the time winter arrived again. Three aircraft were usually parked on a concrete hardstand to facilitate servicing, while the odd blister hanger provided dry if draughty spots for overhauland repair. The Mustangs in these pictures (AG528, AL971 and AP222) have flame damping exhaust stubs which were fitted to 400 Squadron's aircraft at an early date to enable the unit to fly night Ranger operations.

By the end of January 1943 691 Mustangs had arrived in the United Kingdom, fulfilling two orders totalling 620 Mustang Is, and a later order for 150 Mustang IAs with four 20-mm cannon wing armament in place of the eight machine guns of the Mk I. The discrepancy between the number ordered and the delivery, resulted from losses at sea and appropriations by the USAAF. The only other Allison-engined Mustangs received by the RAF was a single example of the A-36 dive-bomber version, ordered for the USAAF in quantity, and 50 P-51As to replace the Mustangs taken over in the USA from the Mk IA order. The P-51A was basically a refined version of the Mustang IA with improved engine performance, wing racks for expendable stores, and four 0.50in calibre machine guns—the weapon preferred by the Americans. In British service these were known as Mustang IIs and they arrived in the United Kingdom in June and July 1943. Thereafter USAAF orders for a re-engined long-range fighter development

of the Mustang occupied production at North American factories, and examples of this later model supplied to the RAF were too few and too precious to allocate to tactical reconnaissance units.

Although the Mustang force of Army Co-operation Command had been reduced to 15 full squadrons by January 1943, normal attrition would eventually lead to further reductions with no compensating shipments forthcoming from the United States. Three squadrons had been sent to North Africa in November 1942, leaving their Mustangs behind to convert the last Tomahawk squadron and equip a new Canadian unit. The accident rate for Mustangs was not extortionate (in comparison with Fighter Command types) but it was a fact that twice as many were wrecked or damaged beyond repair in flying accidents than were ever lost to the enemy. By the summer of 1943 the position was critical and between September that year and January 1944, nine squadrons had to be converted to other

TAC R
Far left: The photographs
that Tac R Mustangs brought
back were usually of Allied
or enemy ground activity.
On 14th August 1944 the
camera of a 168 Squadron
Mustang caught the wingman
in a steep turn against a
background of an advancing
armoured column to make
what is probably the most
graphic picture of the
Tac R mission as executed
in Europe. While the
identities of the indididual
aircraft involved in the
photograph have not been
established, one of the
veteran Mark Is operating
with 168 Sqn that day was
the second Mustang built,
AG346.

COMFORTABLE PERCH
Left: After the deluge that
soaked Eindhoven airfield
in the autumn of 1944,
Corporal George Adams
makes use of a spot of
sunshine on 28th October to
dry his undercarriage.
AL986,P served with 430
Squadron from 4th October
until 4th November when she
sustained flak damage and
was sent to a depot for
repair.

types, some to changed roles.

Army Co-operation Command was disbanded in late June 1943 and its Mustang squadrons transferred first to Fighter Command and later in the year to 2nd Tactical Air Force, the formation being prepared for the cross-channel invasion in the following spring. On D-day five Mustang tactical reconnaissance squadrons remained—Nos. 2, 168, 268, 414 and 430 —and this 100-strong force engaged in intensive operations in support of ground forces during the campaigns that followed, eventually moving to France and through Belgium into Holland. Many of the aircraft used were Mark Is that had left North American's factory three years before. In fact, the first Mustang to arrive in England, AG346—the second machine constructed—served with 168 Squadron until the late summer of 1944.

The low level photographic and visual reconnaissance missions undertaken by these units brought many losses and by January 1945 only 268 Squadron had

Mustangs, chiefly Mk IIs in which it saw out the war in Europe. When in July 1945 the squadron's battered aircraft were finally flown away a three year association was ended. Only one other operational RAF squadron was flying Allison Mustangs at the end of hostilities—No. 26, the first to receive a Mustang back in January 1942. The unit had converted to another type late in 1943 but in October 1944 it reverted to Mustang Is to meet an urgent requirement for low level photographic reconnaissance of possible V-2 rocket launching sites in Holland. Only the Mustang combined the required speed and range for this task. No. 26 Squadron also retained its Mustangs until the end of hostilities but by then less than a hundred Allison versions remained with the RAF. To the end it was unsurpassed for the mission it performed. Indeed much of the technique of tactical reconnaissance, to be invaluable in the final land campaigns of the war, was pioneered in the Allison Mustang.

37

A Rather Special Club

Tom Fazan

I returned to England in the spring of 1942 after service with army co-operation squadrons in the Middle East. After leave I was sent down to Gatwick to take command of 26 Squadron which was then in the process of converting to Mustangs. Having flown Lysanders in the Middle East, the transition to the Mustang seemed a big step. The 'Lizzie' was virtually a spotter plane, manoeuvrable and slow. The Mustang was twice as fast and twice as heavy but I must admit that I had no problems in mastering its ways. Frankly, it was surprisingly docile and I always felt the aircraft was flying me and not me it. It was very stable and I particularly liked the wide track undercarriage which was also appreciated by the older hands in the Squadron who experienced the changeover from Tomahawks. These had a comparatively narrow track and ground loops were not uncommon. The Mustang was also a very solid aircraft; one felt the construction was good and that it would stand up to the rough and tumble of operational use very well—and it did. Although 26 was the first squadron to receive Mustangs we had no real teething troubles with the aircraft and the Allison engine proved very dependable.

In view of the Mustang's later success as a fighter, people tend to think of the aircraft solely in this role; while it was designed as a fighter its original service with the RAF was as a reconnaissance aircraft. We were not trained as fighter pilots neither were we expected to act as fighter pilots: our job was reconnaissance first and foremost and any other forms of operation were ancillary to our primary role. We did attack ground targets but this was really to give us operational experience at a time when there was no land campaign to support.

The army co-operation pilot was quite a different animal from the fighter pilot: he was an independent character, as occasioned by his job. He was very much the loner and the success of any sortie usually depended on the individual and not on a team in Army Co-operation Command ops. We nearly always operated at extremely low altitude for reconnnaissace sorties, and although usually sent out in pairs it was essential for both pilots involved to be thoroughly familiar with the terrain over which they flew to reach the objective. At 50 to 100 feet one could not afford to miss a landmark and become lost, if only temporarily, over hostile country at that height. Every one of these operations was thoroughly planned and executed.

The standing instructions were to evade

enemy aircraft and only protect ourselves when attacked. German fighters would have the element of surprise as we often set a straight course and because of the low altitude at which we flew pilots were too busy concentrating on the problems of navigation to keep an eye out behind. In my opinion we were in more danger of running into trees and other obstructions than we were prone to enemy interception. No one in 26 got involved in a successful combat with Jerry during the year I was in command, although some of the other squadrons did see some action and gave a good account of themselves.

Most of our losses—and they were small in relation to the number of sorties we flew—were to ground fire. Operations were planned to avoid known flak areas but we couldn't miss them all and at 50 feet or less we were inviting targets for any German soldier with a rifle. The element of surprise saved us from a good deal of anti-aircraft fire for by the time the gunner had reached his weapon we were gone. The Dieppe landing was our most costly day when five pilots did not return. But that was a special operation and we were continually exposed to ground fire in the areas where the Army required surveillance.

Army co-operation pilots were probably, on average, a little older than the fighter boys. I'd also say they were more studied, probably because one needed an entirely different approach to the sort of work we were doing. That isn't to say they were less colourful. 26 certainly had its personalities —such as the indomitable 'Slug' Murphy. We also had Aubrey Baring—of the banking family—and Chris 'Kit' North-Lewis, who was to become a high ranking officer in the post-war RAF.

Most of us liked being in Army Co-operation Command; it was like a rather special club. We were sorry when it was disbanded and the squadrons were turned over to Fighter Command. Previously all Mustang squadrons had usually been commanded by a Wing Commander, but one of the first things Fighter Command did was to replace the Wing Commanders with Squadron Leaders.

The Mustang had originally been turned down by Fighter Command but I'm sure they came to think very highly of it, certainly the pilots did. During scheduled practices we encouraged this appreciation through engaging Spitfires in mock dogfights—a very enjoyable sport. Spitfires could out-turn us at any height but we were faster at low-level. We always liked to think we had the edge on them.

Uncle Sam Saddles his Blues

Having produced an outstanding single-engine fighter, it was to be expected that North American Aviation would find a ready buyer in the US Army Air Force. Initially the NA-73 was looked upon as a foreign project and even after the prototype showed such an excellent performance the USAAF took little interest. Two examples from early production were acquired for evaluation under the designation XP-51. Despatched in August and December 1941 to Wright Field, Dayton, Ohio (HQ Material Command and USAAF experimental centre), they were primarily employed in testing special items of equipment and were not immediately evaluated to meet service requirements.

The USAAF had ordered, and was developing, the P-38, P-39, P-40 and P-47. Additionally, the Force was endeavouring to select the best of several other fighter designs of a more radical nature and, understandably, with ample eggs in the basket there was no wish to complicate matters further by adding to the load, besides which this North American egg was doing very well in the British basket. Even so, an Act of Congress had the effect of making the USAAF sponsor orders—if only on paper. British funds for purchasing US war material were running short by late 1940 so in the following March the US Government supplemented Cash and Carry with Lend-Lease. With credit available on this basis the British intensified their buying programme, but before aircraft could be lent and leased a US military agency had to order. To keep the arrangements respectable and within the Act, such aircraft were built ostensibly for the USAAF and given appropriate designations and serial numbers. Thus 150 cannon-armed Mustang IAs ordered for the British in September 1941 were officially built as P-51-NAs.

While not having any great interest in the Mustang, the USAAF constantly reviewed RAF techniques and equipment and came more and more to model preparations on British experience. Very significant were the developments in reconnaissance and air-ground support, and the USAAF was wont to re-equip and train its own observation squadrons along these lines. When on 7th December 1941, the USAAF suddenly became no longer just a friendly and helpful observer to the RAF, but a combatant in the air war, considerations became priorities. British satisfaction with the Mustang and the complimentary opinions of American pilots who had flown the two XP-51s in connection with propeller and gun charging experiments, motivated the USAAF at last to conduct a test programme on the two prototypes. On the strength of the results 55 of the Mustang IAs were diverted to reconnaissance units. These P-51s were modified in much the same way as British Mustangs, with a camera for oblique photography installed directly aft of the cockpit crash brace support. The good behaviour of the Mustang in a dive led North American to offer the USAAF a dive bombing version, fitted with air brakes, capable of carrying two 500lb bombs suspended from wing racks. The RAF and Luftwaffe had converted their fighters to the fighter bomber role with much success, and the USAAF had been particularly impressed by the effectiveness of the Stuka dive-bombers in the 1939 Polish and 1940 French campaigns. Aircraft specifically for this purpose were under development in the States although their performance was not impressive.

North American envisaged that adapting the Mustang to this role could result in a dive-bomber with a vastly superior per-

formance to its contemporaries, while providing a similar range and bomb load. With the laudatory reports on the XP-51 as an added encouragement, the USAAF approved the design study and ordered no less than 500 examples of this Mustang designated the A-36 (A for Attack). As the airframe would be exposed to extra stresses and strains, North American undertook a thorough reappraisal of construction and airframe behaviour. Following wind tunnel tests some modifications resulted, notably to the radiator scoop. Bomb shackles were installed under each wing, outboard of the undercarriage and directly under the machine gun bays. Hydraulically operated lattice type dive brakes were situated one above and below each main plane. The one 0.50 and two 0.30 guns sited in each wing of the British Mustangs, were replaced by two 0.50s to conform with the USAAF's preference for heavier calibre machine guns. The A-36 also featured a refined engine, giving more power at low altitudes, but this did not improve all-round performance appreciably as the A-36 was slightly heavier than the P-51 and the wing racks caused drag.

The first A-36A was completed at Ingle-

wood in September 1942 with production following on after the P-51 order. Further recognition for the Mustang followed with a contract for 1,200 P-51A tactical fighters specifically for the USAAF. The P-51A used the V-1780-81 model Allison which developed full power at 20,000 feet as against 15,000 feet with the earlier P-51. The nose armament was delted to ease engine maintenance and eliminate the complicated and weighty syncronising mechanism; the wing guns were four 0.50s as with the A-36. In fact, the P-51A employed a similar wing to the A-36, with provision for carrying under-wing stores, but without the dive brakes. Fifty of these P-51As were allocated to Britain—where they were known as Mustang IIs—as replacements for the cannon-armed P-51s from the earlier Defence Aid contract appropriated by the USAAF.

The USAAF adopted an official names policy in 1942 under which the P-51 was to be called Apache. By the time the first cannon armed P-51s had been appropriated in July 1942, Apache had been dropped in favour of the British name 'Mustang'. When fitted with a camera for a photographic role the P-51s were offi-cially designated F-6As (F for Photo-graphic) although in practice they were still usually referred to as P-51s. First examples went to the photographic recon-naissance school at Colorado Springs but tactical reconnaissance training with Must-angs eventually settled on Key Field in Mississippi. Anxious to test their P-51s under combat conditions, the USAAF shipped 35 to North Africa where they arrived in March 1943 and were assigned to the 68th Observation Group's 111th and 154th Obs. Sqdns at Oujda, French Morocco. These squadrons had a mixture of P-39s, P-38s and Spitfires; the P-51s were eventually used in the 111th Squad-ron which later became the only USAAF tactical reconnaissance unit operating in the Mediterranean theatre. However, the early combat sorties with P-51s were flown by the 154th Squadron and during a strafing attack by four aircraft on an enemy held road, one was shot down by a US Army battery that mistook the angular newcomer for a Messerschmitt! And this in spite of previous notification that P-51s were in the battle area.

A-36As started reaching USAAF units in October 1942 and four groups were

OLD GLORY TAIL
A P-51 of the small consignment shipped to North Africa and used by the 111th and 154th Tac. Recon. Sqns. Stars and Stripes marking was for the benefit of the local populace who it was believed would be unfamiliar with the identity of the star device. Variable radiator scoops are both full down on this aircraft. Front scoop had a fixed position on later Mustangs.

43

SPECIAL DELIVERY
The A-36A was used on several occasions to deliver supplies to Allied troops fighting over the mountainous terrain in central Italy. Modified drop tanks filled with food or medical requirements were carried on the bomb racks and free dropped. The tank released by the 27th Group A-36 in the photograph contains food for soldiers of the 5th Army 'dug in' on the slopes of Mt. Maggiore: 20th December 1943.

training on the type during the winter months.

There were a number of accidents with the A-36 usually resulting from pilots getting into difficulties during a dive. The approved method of attack was for a pilot to approach his target at around 10,000 feet and when nearly overhead to extend the air brakes and turn into a near vertical dive making release at about 4,000 feet and then pulling out. The air brakes restricted speed built up in the dive, but had a nasty habit of not extending equally due to imbalance of hydraulic pressures. When this occurred it was difficult to keep the aircraft aimed true at its target and there were instances of complete loss of control. Occasionally unrestricted manoeuvres in speed dives caused airframe failure and the aircraft broke up. At one time A-36 training was resulting in the highest accident rate per hour's flying time of any other major combat type in the USAAF. Even so, at a restricted test at the Proving Ground Command Centre at Eglin, Florida in April 1943, one A-36A used shed both wings when its pilot tried to recover from a 450mph dive.

The 86th Bomb Group (with four squadrons) was the first A-36A trained unit deployed overseas, sailing for North Africa in March 1943. Just over three hundred A-36As were available there by late May and many went to re-build the 27th Bomb Group, which arrived with a part complement of Douglas A-20 Havoc light bombers only to have aircraft and crews taken to make good losses in units already in action. The 27th, under Lt.-Col. John Stevenson, entered combat in June by dive-bombing the Axis's island airfield of Pantelleria. This was followed by the invasion of Sicily and the 27th's participation in this invasion led to the adoption of the name Invader for the A-36. The suggestion came from a 27th pilot 'because we keep invading places' and though it caught on in the theatre it was never officially adopted and did not persist beyond the spring of 1944.

The 86th Group joined the 27th in Sicily in July and both groups were actively involved as air support for the invasion of Italy. The excellence of A-36 ground support, especially at attacking enemy gun positions and other strong points holding up the advance of ground forces, earned them high praise.

Although a calamitous official test in the United States had resulted in recommendations that in dive-bombing A-36As the angle of descent be reduced to 70 degrees and, because of inconsistency in operation, the brakes should not be used, the 27th Group kept very much to the original concept of attack. It was found that really accurate bomb delivery could only be achieved with a 90 degree dive on the target. Modifications had largely overcome the dive-brake problems and the brakes were always extended for the near vertical dive. The attack procedure evolved entailed target approach at 8,000 feet— with two 500lb bombs this gave optimum engine performance — extending the brakes, performing a half-roll directly over the target and vertically diving not exceeding 300mph, releasing bombs from 4,000 to 2,000 feet, and recovering from the dive 'on the deck'. Where anti-aircraft fire was intense, the attack was commenced at 10,000 feet and release and recovery made between 5,000 and 4,000 feet, but the course of a dive-bombing attack was so predictable that where sizeable flak defences were encountered a heavy toll was often taken of the A-36As. Each attack element involved a four-plane flight in a follow-the-leader technique which meant that if enemy gunners missed the leaders they were often aligned on the last man down. Tail-end Charlie in an A-36A flight was always a very dangerous job.

The accuracy of many dive-bombing attacks was remarkable. On 31st July 1943, twelve A-36As of the 27th Group were sent against a battery of four heavy guns disrupting the advance of US ground forces in Sicily. A pin-point map location was provided by the army and the A-36A pilots carefully briefed on the terrain in the locality. Having located the spot and circled three times the A-36A pilots were still unable to see the guns, so their leader decided to attack the pin-point reference, an orchard. During and after the attack there was still no sign of the battery or crew, but on return to base a congratulatory message was received from the army stating that all four guns had been put out of action.

Losses began to mount, particularly in the later more static stages of the campaign when German anti-aircraft defences became better organised. By the spring of 1944 half the original A-36 force had been lost and replacements were no longer forthcoming. Both the 27th and 86th Groups, designated as Fighter Bomber Groups in September 1943 and reduced from four to three squadrons apiece, were by this time turning to more general tactical fighter work, engaging in strafing and glide bombing missions which were usually less costly if not so accurate as dive bombing. Over the Salerno beaches, during the Allied landings, the A-36 with a longer loiter time than any other Allied tactical fighter available—about 30 minutes—was in constant use for air cover support. A few A-36As went to the 111th Tactical Recon. Sqdn. (ex-Obs. Sqdn.) to replace P-51 losses, there being no replacements for either model Mustang forthcoming from the USA. The A-36 units were eventually so depleted that the 27th Group was converted to the inferior Curtiss P-40 Warhawk in January 1944, its A-36s being turned over to the 86th which finally had to go over to P-47D Thunderbolts in July. The few A-36s left were retired to Mustang training units until scrapped. The popularity of the A-36 as an aeroplane is evinced by the Twelfth Air Force Commander, Lt.-Gen. John K. Cannon, using one frequently as a personal transport in the Mediterranean theatre.

The only other A-36 trained group to see combat was the 311th which sailed for India by way of Australia in July 1943. As only about forty A-36As were available in India these were assigned to two squadrons of the Group while the third (the 530th) received the first P-51As which had followed the A-36A off the production line. The P-51A was in any case more suited to the operations to which the 311th was generally committed, its mission covering the whole spectrum of tactical combat operations while flying from Dinjan in north-east India: reconnaissance, strafing, dive-bombing, skip-bombing, patrol and interception.

Initially efforts were made to capitalise on the Mustang's range and both P-51As and A-36As were used for the escort of transport and bomber operations. The aircraft's deficiencies in air combat were quickly highlighted when, on their first sorties, to provide cover for transports flying from India to China over 'the Hump', three A-36As were missing, presumed shot down. Notwithstanding the Japanese fighters' known superiority in dog fights, the 530th Squadron with most of its P-51As was detached from the Group and moved south to Kurmitola in Bengal for the express purpose of escorting Mitchells and Liberators during attacks on the Rangoon area. These missions were to be the first really long-range escorts undertaken by Mustangs during the war and they entailed round flights of nearly 900 miles. Two 75 US gallon drop-tanks made this possible but after four such missions the squadron's strength had been halved and more cautious employment followed.

While providing cover for a Mitchell attack on Mingaladon airfield on 25th November, the squadron was surprised by four Oscars (Allied code name for the Nakajima Ki-43 fighter) of the crack 64th Sentai—residents of the airfield under attack. In the ensuing combat, during which the Mustangs engaged in a turning fight at low altitude, two P-51As were shot down with no loss to the enemy. The second of these long distance escorts was even more disastrous. Liberators were shepherded to Insein but the heavily loaded Mustangs could not rise much above the bombers' altitude and near the target they were again surprised by Oscars of the 64th Sentai. One Mustang was sent down in flames before the pilot had time to release his impeding drop tanks. In the following mêlée three other Mustangs were fatally hit, including that of Colonel Harry Melton, the 311th Group commander. One Japanese fighter was shot down by the Mustangs and another crash-landed through damage received in the fight. Finally, on 1st December a Liberator raid on Rangoon found the Mustangs again without altitude advantage and outnumbered. One was lost in an unequal combat and another ran out of fuel on the long trip back to the staging airfield at Cox's Bazaar.

While the P-51A was superior to the P-40 and P-38 for fighter-fighter combat at low and medium altitudes, it was still slower in acceleration and less manoeuvrable than the nimble Oscars and Tojos that were the principal adversaries. Nevertheless, the early misfortunes of the 311th Group were in part due to the inexperience of a new unit facing one very experienced. As a result, P-51A pilots were instructed not to engage in slow turning fights but to make swift attacking passes and to out-distance the enemy before making a 180 degree turn to re-engage: this was and had been standard operational procedure with P-40s and most other Allied types for two years.

All told, some 100 P-51As were sent to India being the final production batches of Allison-engined Mustangs. In addition to the 311th Group they were used by two Air Commando units and a few found their way to USAAF fighter squadrons in China. The Air Commando units were part of the self-contained air support force specially created to serve the incursions of British Major-General Orde Wingate behind enemy lines. This rigorous assignment demanded much of the 30-odd P-51As acquired for ground attack and air defence. Not only were they operating from small rough landing strips but often with exceptionally heavy loads. A 500lb bomb on each wing rack was the maximum recommended load, but Air Commando P-51As were successfully operated with 1,000lb bombs in February 1944. The three-tube Bazooka rocket installation under each wing was another innovation, although these came to be widely used by all Mustang units in the China-India-Burma theatre. Turbulence set up by the rocket tubes affected the pitot tube pressure (due to the proximity of the tube cluster to the pitot head under the right wing) resulting in a 20mph variation in Indicated Air Speed, imposing a need for great care when landing on the short jungle strips.

The Air Commandos employed on occasions the cable dragging technique of bringing down telephone wires. This hazardous process involved taking off with a long wire rope attached at each end to the wing rack release points and trailing out behind the aircraft's empenage. Another length of wire rope with several small steel weights fixed to it was attached at the apex of a loop formed by the first wire rope. Hanging beneath the aircraft in flight the steel balls would demolish telephone wires with ease. The whole apparatus was released over base prior to landing.

By the spring of 1943 the range potential of the Mustang had nearly every US combat theatre clamouring for the type and an acute shortage developed. For the cross-channel invasion of Europe, set for the spring of 1944, the USAAF intended es-

47

PICTURE PACKIN' PLANES

Above: The only Allison engined Mustangs sent to the UK for the USAAF were a small number of F-6Bs (P-51As) which were assembled at Renfrew, Scotland in October 1943. Lockheed operated the organisation employing local fitters under specialist supervision. The aircraft had already been modified to take an oblique camera in the same position as RAF Mustangs. This fitment can be seen in the aircraft being run-up on test (43-6169). The Mustang having its tail assembly installed, 43-6053, was reported Missing In Action on 19th July 1944 and 43-6169 went the same way exactly a month later. Both aircraft were serving with the 107th Tac. Recon. Sqn.

IN THE FIELD

Left: Two F-6B Mustangs of 107th Tac. Recon. Sqn in company with a 'silver' F-6D, on Toussus le Noble airstrip during the Allied advance through France in September 1944.

tablishing a number of P-51A units in the UK. These were to have a tactical reconnaissance mission and the aircraft would be fitted with cameras for oblique photography and used along the lines so successfully evolved by the RAF's Allison Mustangs. But production of these models was being terminated and only two dozen P-51As arrived in the UK and they were delivered to the 67th Reconnaissance Group at Membury in October 1943 to replace its Spitfires. First Popular type sorties were flown by the 107th Squadron on 20th December 1943 and this squadron eventually took charge of all P-51As. Although no further P-51As were received and five were lost in combat, a few endured until the final month of the war.

All told the USAAF received 819 Allison-engined Mustangs (more than the RAF) and pilots who flew the aircraft were enthusiastic in its praise, seemingly to a man—particularly if they had come to the Mustang via some of the more laggardly and temperamental pursuits of those days. The scarcity of P-51s in the States made them jealously guarded by the personnel of the few training fields to which they were assigned. This is clearly obvious in the following account by the then Lt.

Jesse Thompson whose first flight in a Mustang was enlivened by the failure of the airspeed indicator.

"My first flight in a P-51 took place at Zephyr Hills Field (near Dade City, Florida) in the summer of 1943. The aircraft was an early P-51A and that first flight was a thrill in more ways than one. I had previously made a few flights in war-weary P-40s but I was unprepared to see the ASI climb to 80-90mph as I accelerated down the runway and then settle back to zero! Even so, the take-off and climb to altitude was much less unsettling than the excited advice broadcast from the tower after I had unwisely informed them of my problem. After 15 to 20 minutes of argument, I finally convinced them that, if they would just leave me alone, I could practise some stalls and shoot cloud-top landings with the gear and flaps extended and I was confident that I could land their pretty bird with no sweat. Most certainly, I did not want a pace machine to distract my attention while landing a strange bird with no ASI. In the event, as the British say, I was right and made a perfect landing—better than I was ever able to do afterwards."

**DAMN GREAT MERLIN
STICKING OUT IN FRONT**
The Merlin 65 in Mustang
AL975, the first conversion
completed by Rolls-Royce
and flown on 13th October
1942. A special engine
mounting was fabricated for
this aircraft.

A Bit more Poke

In the early days of the war the British Air Ministry were ever mindful of the United States aircraft manufacturers' general tendency to over-state the capabilities of their products. This attitude changed as the years passed, but when the Mustang arrived in England late in 1941, it was the subject of some reservations until flight testing proved it achieved or came close to attaining the attributes of North American and British test pilots in the United States.

By the spring of 1942 several distinguished test pilots had flown the Mustang in the United Kingdom and, almost to a man, were impressed by its handling and performance. For a fighter it was remarkably docile with light control forces and about the only repetitive complaint was weak aileron response. All this was in the context of a medium/low altitude fighter; above 25,000 feet the Allison struggled in the thin air and it would have been foolish to attempt combat at such an altitude. To quote an RAF comment in the parlance of those days, "It's a bloody good aeroplane, laddie; only it needs a bit more poke."

The initial moves in obtaining a 'bit more poke' were made by Rolls-Royce test pilot Ronald Harker. Part of his work was evaluating the performance of aircraft powered by engines from other manufacturers, including American and enemy types as well as those of British competitors. One of his haunts was the Air Fighting Development Unit at Duxford, near Cambridge, where a range of fighter aircraft were continually under test. In April 1942 Harker was invited by the Unit CO at Duxford to fly an early Mustang undergoing suitability trials at the station. On the last day of the month Harker, accompanied by his wife and a Rolls project engineer, set out by car from Hucknall on the four hour journey to Duxford where he spent thirty minutes flying the Mustang. This illuminating experience convinced him that the aircraft had a most advanced and aerodynamically clean airframe and that the laudatory comments he had heard were justified. He was in no doubt about the type's manoeuvrability and speed being superior to the Spitfire V—the standard RAF day fighter—at altitudes below 15,000 feet. A limiting factor, as he saw it, was the fall-off of power above that altitude. But, he surmised, the new two-stage, two-speed supercharged Merlin 61 that had given the latest Spitfire such a performance boost might also do wonders for the Mustang.

Back at Hucknall, Harker asked Rolls' Chief Aerodynamic Engineer, W. O. W. Challier, to work out a set of performance figures for such a combination. Calculations gave a top speed of 441mph—an advance of 70mph on the Allison Mustang's maximum, but more important was the fact that this figure was obtained at 25,600 feet as against 13,000 feet. In several respects this design study credited a Merlin 61-powered version of the Mustang with a performance equal to, or better than, a Spitfire using the same engine. The proposal was put to influential people at Rolls-Royce and the Air Ministry who were also impressed. Official action for experimental conversion of Mustang I airframes to the Merlin was obtained and the work put in hand at Hucknall.

Currently the assistant air attaché at the US Embassy in London was Major 'Tommy' Hitchcock, famous pre-war as a star polo player. Always an adventurer, he had flown with the Lafayette Escadrille in the First World War at the age of 18, had been wounded in an air fight, forced down behind German lines, and later escaped into Switzerland. His interest in fighter aircraft made him a frequent visitor to

MERLIN COMPARISON
Right hand views of the
Rolls-Royce installation of a
Merlin 65 in AL975 (top) and
the Packard Merlin in a
production P-51B.

RAF establishments and in particular the AFDU. Here he was made aware of the RAF's respect for the Mustang and the opinion that, if powered by a Merlin, this aircraft would surpass any other American made fighter. Manufacture of the Merlin in the USA had been arranged during 1940 and by 1942 this engine was in full production at the Packard factory at Detroit. It was being used in Canadian and British aircraft production as well as the Curtiss P-40 for both US and British forces. Moreover, Packard were currently preparing for production a model based on the Merlin 61. To arrange a marriage between the Packard Merlin and the Mustang became something of an obsession for Hitchcock. He took his proposal to his ambassador, John Winant and, armed with the endorsement of several senior RAF officers, managed to obtain an interview with the USAAF's commanding general, 'Hap' Arnold, in Washington. Hitchcock found an ally in Air Marshal Sir John Slessor; together they put the case for the Merlin Mustang to Arnold in his Pentagon office.

Arnold, impressed, if not convinced, preferred to await the outcome of the Rolls-Royce conversion project before making any decisions on large scale production. It should be appreciated that at this date, October 1942, the P-38 Lightning still appeared to meet the USAAF's requirements for a long range escort fighter, while the P-47 Thunderbolt was showing excellent performance at high altitudes. There were problems with both these types and the USAAF did not wish to further complicate the expedition of their development plans nor diversify fighter production programmes more than necessary. Further, the mode of employment of the USAAF's daylight high altitude bombing force had yet to be disproved, in fact, the first few sorties by Fortresses over Europe seemed to indicate that they could very well defend themselves without excessive losses. Probably the biggest factor weighing against the Merlin development of the Mustang was the persisting view of Air Material Command that this aircraft should continue to be developed for ground attack or tactical reconnaissance, not as a fighter.

On Tuesday, 13th October 1942, Rolls' chief test pilot, Captain Ronald Shepherd, flew the Mustang X—as the Merlin conversion aircraft was designated—for the first time. Modifications were necessary to the power plant and airscrew before anything like the estimated performance was attained, but the preliminary flight data, air mailed to Washington and presented to Arnold, was the deciding factor in persuading him to overrule Air Material Command and order large scale procurement of the Mustang as a fighter.

The first Mustang X was built from Mustang I AL975. The engine originally intended for installation was a Merlin 61 as currently fitted to the Spitfire IX. Rolls, however, eventually built a slightly more powerful version, the Merlin 65, specially

for the Mustang, embodying a fuel injection carburettor and new supercharger gear ratios. The compact integral two-stage supercharger was a major factor in giving the Merlin its pronounced ascendancy over the Allison. While the Allison developed maximum power at sea level and after 10,000 feet the power output rapidly declined, the Merlin 65 could maintain its power to 22,000 feet before declivity. At best the Merlin 65 was giving out some extra 600hp over the Allison V-1710-39. The British engine, though over 300lb heavier, was of very similar dimensions to the original power plant and did not offer any great difficulty in installation. Rolls engineers chose to remove the original engine mount and construct a completely new frame to take the Merlin. An intercooler for the supercharged mixture was fed with coolant from a small radiator

NEW BREED
The first production Merlin Mustang as it appeared shortly after leaving the Inglewood line in April 1943. Shortage of engines delayed mass production during the spring and early summer of that year.

placed under the engine. The intake for this also served as the carburettor air scoop, re-positioned from its Allison position above the top cowling. The new nose scoop was a rather large affair, not unlike that of the Curtiss P-40 Kittyhawk and Warhawk spoiling the Mustang's hitherto neat lines. The cooling air entered the engine bay and was released through fixed louvres in the fuselage side just forward of the cockpit.

The Merlin Mustang was distinctly a wilder aircraft to pilot than her predecessor. The powerful engine and four-blade propeller tended to affect directional stability, particularly in a dive, and generally the aircraft required constant control adjustments to keep trimmed. The Allison Mustang had been so positively pleasant to fly, that pilots had tended to consider the design almost perfect from an aerodynamic

viewpoint; so that a pilot familiar with the old order, was startled by the new. The rasping, crackling, ear-shattering roar of the Merlin and the occasional shudder that it sent through the airframe were not well received by the pilot used to sitting behind the comparatively docile Allison. In short, the Merlin Mustang was not such a pleasant aeroplane to fly as its predecessor but its combat potential was unquestionably far superior. Four other Mustang I airframes were fitted with Merlins for experimental purposes, each differed slightly from the others, and were subjected to continual modifications during the winter of 1942/43 and the following spring. Two were eventually turned over to the USAAF in England for evaluation. A top speed of 433mph was eventually obtained and Mustang X could climb to 20,000 feet in 6.3 minutes against 9.1 for Mustang I.

WHOOPS!
Two of the Mustangs converted to Merlins by Rolls-Royce were turned over to the USAAF in the UK and evaluated at Bovingdon. Sudden engine surge is believed to have caused AM121 to nose over on a perimeter track. The wooden propeller blades prevented serious damage to the engine.

Information on the Rolls-Royce Mustang X experiments was sent to North American who, influenced by early British opinion, had already received a contract from the USAAF to install Packard Merlins in two P-51s. These were at first given a completely new pursuit designation, XP-78 but the official body, delighting in confusing nomenclature, had a change of heart and re-designated the prototypes XP-51B. Work on the first, commencing September 1942, was completed late the following month. Schmued and the design team found they could squeeze the Merlin into the existing engine mount with few alterations and while moving the air intake for the updraught carburettor beneath the nose, like Mustang X, and by repositioning the inter-cooler radiator alongside that of the main coolant radiator in the ventral fairing, they were able to produce a small scoop blending into the contours of the cowling and giving a far more streamlined appearance than on the British conversion. Increased radiator capacity was also provided with redesign of the ventral scoop.

The XP-51B made its initial flight on 30th November 1942 with test pilot Robert Chilton at the controls. The aircraft behaved as expected except that Chilton was forced to terminate his programme rather hurriedly when the engine started to overheat. A scale-clogged radiator was found, but the reason for this was not so apparent. A new radiator, omitting unreliable materials, had to be manufactured and installed before the test programme could get under way. Although test flying did not resume until late December, on the showing of the first flight and the performance of Mustang Xs in England, an order for Merlin Mustangs was at last approved on 28th December 1942. It would be June 1943 before production of Merlin Mustangs would come from the Inglewood factory, while in August that year the North American factory at Dallas, Texas, previously engaged on other types would also manufacture Mustangs. Models from Inglewood were P-51Bs and those from Dallas P-51Cs. A delay in stepping up Packard production led to many airframes waiting four to six weeks for a power plant during June and July 1943.

For Tommy Hitchcock there was personal satisfaction in seeing the aircraft achieve such prominence in USAAF plans. As time would tell, his enthusiasm was not misplaced, the Mustang arrived only in the nick of time to save the ailing US daylight bomber campaign. Hitchcock, wishing to command a Mustang group, was given the 408th Fighter Group in Texas which he hoped to take overseas with the P-51B. Regrettably for him, the group was assigned to training replacements and only received a few Mustangs. Hitchcock returned to England to serve on the staff of the Ninth Air Force. On 18th April 1944, he was flying a Mustang when, during a high speed dive, both wings broke off, the aircraft crashing near Salisbury. Tommy Hitchcock was killed by the fighter he had promoted. Even so, his death brought to light a hazard which, had it not been discovered, would undoubtedly have claimed other lives.

In view of Hitchcock's experience in test flying, a very detailed examination of the Mustang's wreckage was made, and eventually the cause of the disaster was established. During the fatal dive, when very high speeds had been reached, the large ammunition bay doors on each wing began to bulge outwards. This gave a distorted aerofoil with extreme lift pressures; the strain was too great and the wings tore away. A strengthening of the ammunition bay doors was put in hand and diving limitations imposed. But, to quote Edgar Schmued: "We (the Mustang and North American) had lost a good friend."

The Pioneer Group

The First Operational Merlin Mustang Station: Boxted, England

ALL SOCKED IN
Top: The expression for a seemingly endless undercast like that over which 43-12216,AJ:U, an original P-51B of 356th FS, is flying. Navigation had to be spot on in such conditions and the radio was the vital life-line to home.

THOSE DAMN COOLANT LEAKS
Above: Crew Chief learns 'what's wrong' while other members of 'Suga's' (43-6764,GQ:E) ground crew inspect the clusters of coolant pipes under the engine. Hose joints were prone to leak after prolonged flights and extreme changes of temperature.

LIFT OFF
Right: A P-51B took-off best in a tail-down attitude and needed right rudder during the run to counteract a tendency to swing left—caused by the powerful bite of the four-blade prop. Without external stores a P-51B would come unstuck in 600 yards but with bombs or drop tanks the practice was to hold her down for most of the runway to get plenty of speed. These 355th FS aircraft coming off the north-west Boxted runway are each carrying two 250 lb bombs. The wheel-well fairing doors are coming down on the lead aircraft as the first stage in retraction of the undercarriage.

HOME
Left: While the Crew Chief hears how it went from a weary pilot, fuel tanks are immediately replenished to prevent condensation. In the background another Mustang approaches the runway after an escort to Frankfurt on 29th Jan 1944.

POISED
Lower left: Tail wheel locked, brakes on, left hand on throttle; the pilot of a 355th FS P-51B watches his element leader for the signal to commence the take-off run down a Boxted runway. GQ:M was the personal aircraft of Lt Charles Gumm who became the first Merlin Mustang ace when he shot down his fifth enemy aircraft on 11th February 1944. Tragically, Gumm was killed in a flying accident three weeks later. His aircraft developed engine trouble shortly after take-off and while trying to crash-land on a water meadow near the village of Nayland the Mustang hit a tree with disastrous results.

NEAR THING
Below: Crew Chief S/Sgt William Miller, 356th FS, pokes a finger through the hole in the canopy made by a bullet from a German fighter during a battle near Hanover on 22nd Feb 1944. The bullet tore through the shoulder of pilot Lt Robert Weldon's flying clothes and ripped his shirt but left him unscathed.

GUNS THAT MADE AN ACE

Above: The right-hand gun bay of Charles Gumm's P-51B showing the canted sit of the two Point Fifties. The sharp angle at which belt ammunition was fed into each weapon can be gauged from the shape of the empty feed chutes. The electrical components behind the chutes are gun heaters, necessary at high altitudes if the firing mechanism was to operate efficiently. Even so the heaters could not cope with the extreme temperatures sometimes encountered.

POLISH PAIR

Below: Discussing the troublesome ammunition feeds with an armourer are two Polish pilots. They got themselves 'detached' from the RAF with the idea of flying Mustangs with the 354th Group but competition was too great. Witold Lanowski (right) finally managed to get into the cockpit of a Thunderbolt to fly with the USAAF.

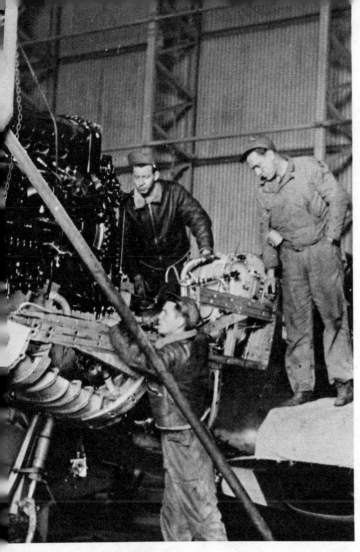

FINGERS!
Above: The tricky job of
hoisting a Merlin—it weighed
1,700 lb—during an engine
change in No 1 hangar at
Boxted. The 'life' of an
engine was reckoned as 200
hours but a Merlin in one of
the early P-51Bs at Boxted
passed the 300 mark before
it was removed.

TINKERING
Left: S/Sgt George Leonard,
Crew Chief, and Sgt Bob
Seager, Assistant Crew Chief
on Charles Gumm's 43-12410,
'tune up' the fuel system—
albeit for Press photographers
at Boxted in January 1944.

A KILL
Right: Final moments of an
Me 110. Pursued by two
354th Group P-51Bs it tried to
escape by coming down to
treetop level. Gun camera film
shows one of the attackers
overshooting the
Messerschmitt as it streams
fire from the right engine
and—a fraction of a second
later—explodes in the snow
covered fields.

Pioneer Personalities

IN THE LAP OF THE GODS
Above: A happy group of
353rd FS pilots outside No 2
hangar at Boxted, 27th
January 1944. L to R: Lt.
Wah Kong, Capt. Wallace
Emmer, Capt. Don Beer-
bower, Capt. Jack Bradley,
Lt. James Parsons and Capt.
James Cannon. Fate,
inevitably, dealt a cruel hand
to some and a kind one to
others. Kong, Emmer,
Beerbower and Parsons were
killed, Emmer and Beer-
bower being two of the
squadron's top scoring pilots
with 14 and 15½ air victories
respectively. Bradley shot
down 15 enemy aircraft—
'M for Margie' was his
personal aircraft.
DING HAO!
Right: A Chinese expression
of luck, six Japanese and six
Nazi symbols were painted
on P-51B 43-6315 by S/Sgt
Marcus Hanson, whose skill
with a paint brush found him
much in demand as a

decorator of aircraft in his
squadron, the 356th. James
Howard's Mustang had a
particular claim to fame.
Flying this aircraft on 11th
January 1944, Howard, then
CO of 356th FS, took on the
protection of an isolated B-17
formation deep in Germany.
His performance in driving
away enemy fighters single-
handed so impressed the
bomber crewmen that he was
later awarded the Medal of
Honor. This highest of US
awards for bravery was the
only one made to a fighter
pilot for air combat over
Europe. Howard had
previously flown with the
American Volunteer Group
in China and then with the
US Navy for the carriers
Lexington, Wasp and *Enterprise*
in the early actions with the
Japanese. He was 6ft 2in tall
and to make himself fit
more comfortably into his
Mustang the rudder pedals
had to be moved forward
and the seat fully back.

VICTORY GRIN
Left: Tired, stiff, sore and with stubble shadow on his chin, Lt. Glenn Eagleston back at Boxted after the first USAAF raid on Berlin. He shot down an Me 109 on this mission to become the 354th's ninth ace. Eagleston flew two tours with the 354th and destroyed a total of 18½ enemy aircraft to become the Group's and the Ninth Air Force's top ace. On one early operation his Mustang was attacked in error by a P-47 and so badly shot up that he had to bale out on return to England.

THE OLD MAN
Left: Lt. Col. Kenneth R. Martin, aged 27, original commander of the 354th Fighter Group. He collided with an Me 109 on 11th February 1944 and spent the rest of the war in a POW camp.

THREE MAJORS
Below: James Howard, (aged 30), George Bickell (27) and Owen Seamen (27), original C.O.s of the 356th, 355th and 353rd Squadrons that made up the 354th Group. All had combat experience in the Pacific air war before coming to Europe. Seamen was lost in the North Sea on 16th December 1943, a victim of engine failure. When Martin went down Howard took over the group until given another assignment in April 1944; Bickell then became group C.O. and remained until the end of the War.

Achtung Mustang!

October 1943 was a crucial time for the US air forces committed to the strategic bombardment of Germany's war industries. Some long range unescorted daylight raids by large numbers of B-17 Fortresses and B-24 Liberators operating from the UK were incurring a 10% loss above which raids were judged prohibitive. Leaders and tacticians who had prompted the campaign, were faced with indisputable evidence that however heavily armed and closely-packed formations of bombers were, they could not adequately protect themselves against concentrated attacks by Luftwaffe fighters. The solution was long-range escorts to keep the enemy fighters at bay. P-47 Thunderbolts had been flying with some success in this role since July, but even with long-range tanks their radius of action of about 350 miles only allowed escort to bombers operating from England to western Germany.

The twin-engined P-38 Lightning, which could reach 450 miles from base, was then considered. P-38 units for the UK already had priority in training and equipment, and two groups were ready for operations. Unfortunately, the aircraft proved disappointing, being hampered by frequent engine failures while on high altitude flights; it became apparent that hopes of the P-38 turning the tide of battle were misplaced. But also in October 1943, P-51Bs, the first production Merlin Mustangs, were being assembled in England and offered an escort fighter potentially far superior to any other single-seat fighter of the day.

Despite agitation to get the Merlin Mustang into production as a high performance fighter, somewhere in the labyrinth of USAAF policy offices there was a body of opinion that regarded the aircraft only as a tactical fighter, performing the same role as the A-36A and early P-51s

Thus the first P-51Bs sent to the UK were assigned to units of the Ninth Air Force, the tactical force preparing to support the land armies in the forthcoming invasion of the European continent. To the worried leaders of the strategic Eighth Air Force, watching the daily losses of their bombers mount, this was a major blunder. There ensued an inter-command haggle over Mustangs and the future of the first three groups to be given the type.

The unit selected to take the new Mustang into combat was the 354th Fighter Group, trained in tactical fighter tactics with P-39 Airacobras. None of its pilots had trained in the older P-51s and most had not seen a Mustang until they arrived at Greenham Common in Berkshire, a large Ninth Air Force service base. Squadron commanders and some headquarters officers had combat experience in the Pacific theatre, but most of the original pilot complement were fresh out of flying schools before joining the 354th during its training with Airacobras in the States.

Operational control of the 354th was initially vested in VIII Fighter Command, as the Ninth Air Force had only just been established in the UK and lacked such facilities. Thus, while the Eighth Air Force could not for the moment obtain P-51Bs for its own units, an opportunity arose to employ those of the Ninth in its service. To raise their experience level, a dozen experienced pilots who had flown Spitfires with US or RCAF squadrons were assigned to the Group and an extremely intensive programme of flight familiarisation and instruction in theatre operational procedures was implemented.

Operational base for the first Merlin Mustangs was Boxted airfield, a few miles north of Colchester, oldest town in Britain. The Group arrived in mid-November and immediately engaged in simulated missions to hasten combat readiness. Experienced VIII Fighter Command officers were at hand to advise and by the end of the month Lt.-Col. Martin, commanding the 354th, was able to advise General Brereton, Commander of the Ninth, that the Group would be operational by 1st December. One of the Eighth Air Force pilots detailed to give the 354th the benefit of his experience was Major Donald Blakeslee, a veteran of the RAF Eagle Squadrons and currently a headquarters pilot with the USAAF's successor to that distinguished band, the 4th Fighter Group. It was Blakeslee who led two twelve-plane formations of P-51Bs from Boxted on the inaugural operation, a sweep over the Belgian and French coasts, a regular familiarisation route for new units.

This mission was uneventful as was the next, a limited escort of B-17s over northern France. The Eighth Air Force was intent on making the maximum use of the P-51B's range and by 11th December enough 75 US gallon drop tanks were available, plus the necessary pressurised plumbing on the aircraft, to enable three dozen Mustangs to fly all the way to Emden to support Fortresses bombing that port. Enemy aircraft were observed by the fighter pilots for the first time, but no engagements ensued. Two days later the 354th flew to the limit of their endurance with 75 gallon tanks—480 miles—from Boxted to watch over B-17s bombing Kiel. Here Me 110 pilots must have been greatly surprised to be opposed by single-engined US fighters. Lt. Glenn Eagleston managed to intercept and fire at one as it dived away, hitting its starboard engine, but was adjudged only to have damaged the enemy.

On 16th December Lt. Charles F. Gumm of 355th Fighter Squadron shot down a Me 110 over Bremen making the first confirmed victory for the Group.

Back over Bremen four days later the three squadrons of the 354th found numbers of Me 110s preparing to attack the bombers with rockets. This time the Mustang pilots were able to claim three destroyed plus a probable, but on the debit side three of their fighters failed to return. This made a total of five missing in action in six missions, and as far as was known all had succumbed to mechanical failure.

The round 800-1000 mile flights of four to five hours' endurance were then extraordinary distances for single engined fighters to cover; amazing, among others, Hermann Goering. For the pilot, cramped in a comparatively small cockpit, much of the time on oxygen, navigating across seemingly endless cloud undercasts, these flights demanded a great deal of stamin and these young men understandably arrived back at Boxted utterly weary. Some authorities argued that this was asking too much of a pilot and placing him at too great a risk on long over-water flights. It was, however, quickly apparent to the US commanders that the presence of friendly fighters over a target meant fewer bombers lost to enemy fighters, and the Mustang was the only single-seat fighter that could engage the enemy on equal terms over the really distant targets. Major General William Kepner, boss of VIII Fighter Command, had seen enough of the Mustang's qualities in these first few missions to say that the P-51B was, "distinctly the best fighter that we can get over here . . . they are going to be the only satisfactory answer."

Nevertheless, the P-51B was not without its troubles, as evidenced by the five aircraft lost on early missions through causes other than enemy action. The Mustang airframe was well tried at low and medium altitudes but the minus temperatures at 25,000 to 30,000 feet above Europe pre-

ACE'S TECHNIQUE

The 4th Group had a particularly successful period of air combat in March and April 1944, and produced a number of high scoring pilots. Two of the leaders were Captains Don Gentile and Duane Beeson, both former members of the RAF Eagle Squadrons. The gun button on RAF fighters was on top of the stick and a preference for this location led the 4th FG to re-wire the stick on Mustangs so that the forward trigger released drop tanks or bombs and the button on top of the stick fired the guns, whereas the reverse was the case on Mustangs serving with other units. Duane Beeson, a master of deflection shooting, kept both hands on the stick when firing, using the left-hand thumb to depress the button. Gentile preferred to keep only his right hand on the stick and use his left for manipulating the throttle. Beeson was shot down while strafing in April 1944.

sented an environment uncongenial to some of its functions. Windshield heating proved insufficient and frost obstructed vision. Coolant leaks occurred and the original sparking plugs quickly fouled up due to the retarded engine setting necessary to conserve fuel on the long flights out to rendezvous with the bombers. Remedies were soon found for these troubles but not so easily cured was the persistent jamming of guns during combat.

The four 0.50 inch machine guns of the P-51B was a meagre armament compared with that of its contemporaries—the P-47 Thunderbolt had double the number of 'point fifties'. A gun stoppage, therefore, presented a serious reduction in firepower, and jams with P-51B guns were frequent and often involved three and sometimes all weapons! Analysis of actions where gun jamming occurred soon highlighted the fact that the trouble happened when guns were fired during tight turns. It was found that when centrifugal forces built up to $1\frac{1}{2}$ or 2G in a tight manoeuvre this

momentarily held back the ammunition belt causing the breech mechanism to block. The trouble was often further complicated by congealed oil if the electrical gun heaters were not switched on some time before firing the guns. An ammunition belt booster motor, as used to feed rounds to some bomber turrets, was the answer and successful applications were made to a number of Mustangs at Boxted. Ideally a repositioning of the guns (they had an angled seating), feed chutes and magazines was required.

To give the Mustang even longer endurance, an 85 US gallon tank had been devised in the US and was being fitted in early P-51Bs at UK depots during December. Later P-51Bs had these tanks installed at the factory and these models were reaching the 354th in increasing numbers by the end of the year. The tank, fitted directly aft of the pilot's seat below the radio equipment, affected the aircraft's centre of gravity and therefore its stability when full, to the extent that it was

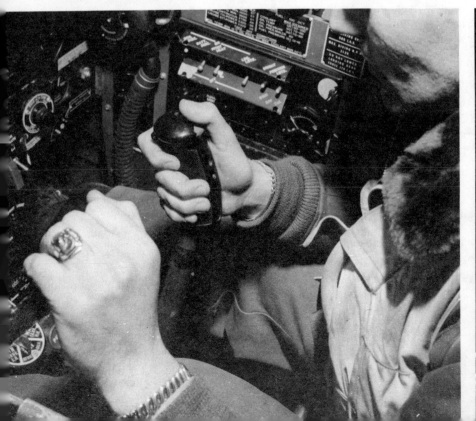

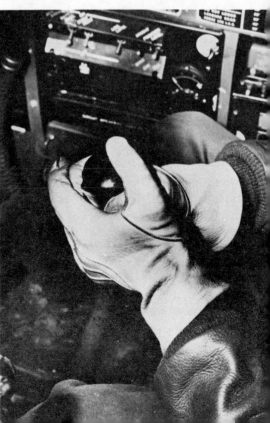

a standing order to draw fuel from this tank immediately after take-off and not to engage in any forceful manoeuvres until over two thirds had been used.

Despite the technical difficulties of early 1944 the 354th went from strength to strength as experience mounted and tactics improved. Over Kiel on 5th January they decimated a Gruppe of Me 110s returning with claims of 18 enemy destroyed for no losses. Six days later 15 claims were credited for no losses during furious battles in the vicinity of Oschersleben and Halberstadt.

The Group did not have all actions in its favour; there were the exceptions when the Luftwaffe had the advantage and scored against the Group. There was, however, another danger, the old bogey of the Mustang looking like the Me 109 and on several occasions Mustangs were attacked by friendly aircraft. To prevent such occurrences white identification bands were painted around the nose and across the flying surfaces of each aircraft. Even this did not stop such incidents. In an air battle near Brunswick on 10th February 1944 a Thunderbolt blazed away at a supposed Me 109 discovering too late its true identity. The Mustang, with shattered instruments and an oil leak, managed to make the perilous crossing of the North Sea but was too badly damaged for the pilot to attempt a landing approach through the clouds so he took to his parachute and came safely down in England. Had the P-47 pilot continued his fire, the Ninth Air Force would have been deprived of Glenn Eagleston, ultimately its highest scoring fighter ace.

The following day Col. Martin, the 354th's CO, was lost. His Mustang collided with an Me 109 and although sustaining severe injuries to a foot, leg and arm, he was thrown clear and managed to open his parachute. He ended up in a German hospital ward alongside the German pilot involved in the incident. Against the loss of the CO and another pilot, the Group made 14 victories and those of Lt. Gumm, Bradley, Turner and Beerbower made them aces.

11th February also marked the operational debut of the second P-51B group, the 357th based at Leiston in Suffolk. This group and the 363rd together with the 354th comprised the Ninth Air Force's Mustang force. The Eighth Air Force, unable to get the 354th transferred to its command, settled for the untried 357th which it exchanged for an operational P-47 group at the end of January. Although largely composed of freshly trained fighter pilots the 357th was flying deep penetration escorts for the bombers within a few days.

P-51B production destined for the RAF were known as Mustang IIIs and those received late in 1943 went to 122 Wing at Gravesend, Kent. This wing was composed of Nos. 19, 65 and 122 Squadrons all formerly equipped with Spitfires. An RAF fighter wing corresponded to a USAAF fighter group although at this stage of the war the American squadron aircraft complement was larger—around 25 as against 16. The early British Mustang IIIs lacked the extra 85 gallon fuselage tank so that their endurance was inferior to those serving with US squadrons. At this time the RAF did not have a pressing long-range fighter requirement of its own and the US squadrons had priority even to the extent of receiving some of the British aircraft in lieu of P-51Bs. Such was the pressing need for more long-range escort, for the large forces of B-17s and B-24s that were then involved in an intensified campaign against the sources of German aircraft production, that the USAAF requested the RAF's

GOODY AND THE KID

Above: Two other 4th Group pilots who ran up high scores during the spring of 1944 were Major James Goodson and Lt. Ralph Hofer, both having 15 air victories by June. Goodson (seated in his P-51B, 43-24848,VF:B) had also destroyed 15 enemy aircraft by shooting them up on enemy airfields, extremely hazardous work. He was eventually shot down by flak while ground strafing but escaped with his life. 'Kid' Hofer was not so lucky and on the first shuttle missions to Russia and Italy was shot down and killed in air combat over the Balkans.

70

FORTUNES OF WAR
Left: P-51Bs at Speke awaiting delivery. Most went to the 4th Fighter Group in late February 1944. Of the two craft in the foreground, 43-6656 was destroyed ten days after this photograph was taken when it flicked over on landing, killing the pilot. 43-6959 flew many missions before failing to return on 11th September 1944.

ACE'S EXIT
Far left/left/Below: Don Gentile finished his combat tour on Thursday 13th April 1944 with a celebration 'buzz job' over Debden. Unfortunately he came in a little too low, his aircraft striking the ground and causing him to belly it in on a neighbouring field a few moments later. The once immaculate 'Shangri-La', sporting 30 victory symbols (Gentile was then credited with 23 air and 7 ground kills) lay with her back broken but Gentile escaped shaken but unhurt. The severed fuselage exposes the two oxygen bottles which gave 3½ to 4 hours supply to a pilot.

Mustang III squadrons fly in support of these missions.

The Mustang III naturally suffered from the same troubles that had bothered the 354th Group at Boxted. Additionally the marrying of British pilot oxygen equipment to the US system in the Mustang needed some minor modifications. It was also noticed that the propeller shaft had a tendency to throw oil and this was attributed to poor seals aggravated by the RAF practice of diluting lubricant with fuel to achieve easier starting in cold weather. No. 65 Squadron received the first Mustang IIIs in December 1943 and an early complaint from pilots was the lack of visibility and restriction of head movement by the canopy. Vision forward and downwards was good but a fighter pilot needed to look to the rear too. In response to this grumble a bulbous one-piece sliding canopy, similar to that of the Spitfire, was experimentally fitted to a Mustang at Boscombe Down, and proving eminently successful was hastened into production. Nearly all RAF Mustang IIIs were eventually fitted with these canopies—known as Malcolm hoods, after the designer—and a great many were also used on USAAF P-51Bs and Cs in Europe. The Gravesend Wing aircraft received theirs in February 1944.

The first RAF Mustang III combat sorties were flown on 15th February 1944 when 19 and 65 Squadrons flew a morning sweep over the enemy-held Channel coast. In the afternoon the two squadrons were out again to escort US heavies bombing V-sites in the Pas de Calais area. Regular escort duties with US bomber formations followed during the next few weeks. Tragedy struck 65 Squadron on 28th February when their CO, Sqn. Ldr. J. C. Grant, a New Zealander, was killed. His Mustang was at 2,500 feet after take-off when the engine failed. Grant glided down as if to make a wheels-up landing but for some reason baled out when only about 300 feet from the ground. His parachute did not have time to fully open.

Penetration increased during March and on the Berlin mission of the 8th, RAF Mustangs flew to meet returning bombers 120 miles west of the German capital. The British contribution was never more than three dozen Mustangs on these operations and they were rarely situated to engage enemy fighters, although they did chase them away from the US formations on a number of occasions. By April, when the US Mustang force had grown to several hundred aircraft, the RAF squadrons were switched to operations of a more tactical nature.

The third USAAF Mustang group, the 363rd based at Rivenhall, Essex, became operational on 22nd February and by 25th the Eighth Air Force's oldest unit, the 4th F.G. at Debden, Essex, had performed '24 hour' conversion from Thunderbolts. This was due to the impetuous Don Blakeslee their commander who, having developed a passion for the Mustang when breaking in the 354th and 357th Groups, talked VIII Fighter Command's General Kepner into giving the 4th P-51Bs with a promise of having them on operations in 24 hours. The 4th became the star performer with the Mustang during March and amassed a fantastic number of victories with its red-nosed fighters. Colourful personalities like Duane Beeson and Don Gentile, both of whom had started their combat with Spitfires, emerged as high-scoring aces in only a few weeks of intense combat. Not all actions resulted in great victories; the reverse did occur, but rarely. On 4th March the squadrons of the novice 363rd Group became separated in the extremely bad weather *en route* to Berlin.

Apparently the Group was lost near Hamburg among the cloud tops extending up to 28,000 feet, when the German raid tracking service vectored a Gruppe of Me 109s to intercept. The German unit, the elite I/JG 1, was able to stalk and surprise the 363rd Group and in the ensuing combat 11 Mustangs were shot down: at least that number did not return, although Luftwaffe claims were 12.

Round trips of twelve hundred miles for the Mustang pilots were now a regular feature as the dismayed Luftwaffe were discovering. Faced with a single-seat fighter of equal calibre to their own interceptors, ranging over most areas of the Reich, the Luftwaffe was caught off guard and overwhelmed. The twin-engined 'destroyers' with which it hoped to deal effectively with the four-engined bombers were particularly vulnerable to this new development. In March and April of 1944 the Luftwaffe's fighter defence force was defeated over its home ground, partly by force of numbers and superior equipment, and partly by superior tactics, but not least by being outfought. The three to four hundred Mustangs played a paramount part in this victory.

An insight into the scope and problems of these Mustang combats can be found in the verbatim accounts made by pilots on their return from operations. That following is not untypical, although Willard Millikan was a very distinguished pilot, formerly with an Eagle Squadron and schooled in the RAF's technique of deflection shooting. It should first be explained that *Horseback* was the radio call sign for the leader of the 4th Group; *Becky*, *Caboose* and *Cobweb* those of his three squadrons. The three or four flights of four aircraft each that made up a squadron formation were identified by different colours and the individual aircraft within

each flight by position numbers. His report reads:

4th FG Combat report for:
1/Lt. Willard W. Millikan, 336 FS.
22nd April, 1944—1800 to 1825hrs—Around a lake at the village of Sachssenhausen S.W. of Kassel, Gr.—Very clear, visibility unlimited; Horseback was leading the Grp. with our squadron-3 sections of four. I was leading Becky Red Flight and was in position on the port with Blue Flight on the starboard led by Lt. Carlson. Passing N. of Hamm at 25,000 feet we let down toward the S.E. to about 18,000 feet when approx. 20-plus Huns were seen orbiting and forming up near the lake. Immediately Horseback called for a starboard orbit and at the same time instructed Caboose and Cobweb squadrons to orbit and the Grp. successfully boxed in the gaggle of Jerries so they had to continue their Lufbery. Going down steeply we circled around starboard to the N. and dropped tanks W. of the lake and then lost sight of the Huns. However Caboose sqd's leader reported he was at 8,000 feet and the Huns were at 5,000 feet at 9 o'clock, so we climbed back up (we had lowered down to 6 or 7,000 feet by this time) and when we reached about 10,000 feet we sighted the e/a off to our left at 9 o'clock. Our sqdr. approached them and flew alongside the circle, my section between Horseback and the Huns. Our 3 sections were all well up, very nearly abreast, and were compact, thus preventing any lagging. I watched the 109s as we flew along and presently one detached himself to attack my section. I called a break to port into his attack and the flight did a beautiful job of breaking and staying together. The Hun kept up his attack and turned steeply to come in on my number 4 man's tail, so I pushed everything forward and dropped

flaps to turn inside him. Through the early stages of the turn he outturned me, but I pulled up and corkscrewed inside him and laid off a deflection shot which hit him hard enough to cause him to flick out of his turn. He started to split-ess but my shots forced him to turn back the other way. Immediately I managed to get a few scattered strikes and he began to skid and slow up and prepare to bale out. I was closing in very rapidly so I dropped full flaps and throttled back completely. I was still overshooting him though so I skidded and raked him without using my sights, for I could not hold my head behind the sight with such violent skids and since I was so close, probably I could not have hit him with sights. Finally I had to break-away over him, and just then he baled out. I wish I could have hit the pilot for he was extremely good and his loss would have meant a lot for our cause. Fortunately I had my flight behind me all the time or I would not have been able to deal with him so successfully. Pulling up and around to port, I reassembled my section and then I saw an Me 109 chasing a Mustang and I jumped him. I had to use a lot of deflection again, blacking out in one of the turns. Luckily I hit him in the turns and caused him to jink trying to avoid my fire and I hit him pretty well again causing him to start smoking and go into a steep dive. I first claimed this one as damaged, for I did not see him crash, but my wingman confirms this one as destroyed. I had to break away for an Me 109 was coming in at me and I could not see what happened. Fortunately for me my No. 3, Lt. Norley, was on hand and did a good job of shooting the devil out of the Me 109 and the Hun went straight in. He was pulling enough deflection on me to shoot me down a dozen times. Turning on around, I pulled up on another Hun and managed to clobber him

in pretty good shape after turning and pulling and doing awful things to the engine. I got strikes with a deflection shot and I would have to pull my nose through, fire a short burst, let off my turn so I could see the Hun, and then pull through again. I managed to get scattered strikes this way and the Hun half-rolled and went straight in. By this time things were certainly mixed up, and it seemed we had been fighting for hours. Fires were burning everywhere and all the fighting had taken place from 8,000 feet on down to the deck. Pulling around again, I sighted another Me 109 and I tackled him, but he put up an amazing demonstration of aerobatics, and I soon found myself alone. I again laid

off deflection and hit him and he straightened out and slow-rolled. I shot again and hit him just as he rolled out of it. Immediately he rolled on his back and ploughed into the ground at a flat angle. He was burning pretty well and I must have hit the pilot. I started to follow when he half-rolled but realised I was only 1,500 feet up and I recovered right over the tree tops. I pulled up and around to port again and looked for another Hun after I had made sure I was clear of Huns behind me. I sighted another Me 109 gliding into a field streaming glycol from his engine. I dove immediately and attacked him from starboard, about 5 o'clock to the Hun and at the same time a Mustang on his tail was

coming in pretty fast. I laid off about a ring of deflection and shot just over him on his left, and at the same time the Mustang on his tail was shooting up the ground in front of him. I don't think I hit him in this dive and I believe whoever was behind him shot him up the most. Pulling up again the boys tried to reorganise, and I was rejoined by my No. 3, Lt. Norley and Lt. Godfrey. Seeing several of the boys circling around aimlessly I asked them to join up with me and I was able to get nine of us all together. Several of the boys were complaining of engine trouble and one or two complained that their electrical systems were shot, so I said we would head out after getting permission from Horseback to

MAN O'WAR

The appropriate nickname given by Cliborne Kinnard to the five Mustangs he used up during a year's combat flying with the Eighth Air Force. This was the first (43-6431;WR:A) which he flew with the 354th FS, 355th FG from Steeple Morden. The squadron dubbed itself 'The Bulldogs' after the subject of its official badge. Kinnard was the unit's No 1, hence the inscription on the Mustang's nose. Kinnard commanded two fighter groups during his second tour in Europe. He was credited with destroying 8 aircraft in air combat and 17 by strafing.

SWEATING 'EM IN SUMMER
Here she comes, 105 mph IAS over the fence on a nice approach. A crew chief at Bottisham keeps a critical eye on a metal finish P-51B of the 375th FS returning from a D-Day mission. Silver drop tanks are 'paper' 108 US gallon and metal 75 US gallon types. Bottisham was a grass field with steel mesh mat runways. Fine on a sunny June day but unpleasantly muddy in winter.

take the boys home. Around Hamm we could see all the bombers coming in, and there was ample fighter protection—P-38s, 47s and I believe some Mustangs other than ours, but I was too far away to identify these for sure. There were several things that made this mission such a success and I think they are important. One was that our sqdr. was very well together, sections were compact and well up on the leading section, and our wingmen stayed with their number one men—I could not have done a thing without the close co-operation and assistance of every man in the section. They gave me the necessary cover and moral support when I was chasing a Hun and I was able to spend

more time concentrating on shooting and manoeuvring. Lt. Patteeuw, my wingman, was on his fourth trip, and he did an excellent job of staying with me. When he did lose me it was purely accidental, and I don't think anyone could have stayed with me under the circumstances. Lt. Logan flying on Horseback's wing stuck with him through the whole flight, and when Lt. Patteeuw separated from me he immediately joined up with Horseback. Good wingmen are at a premium, and without them we could not do much. The Huns seemed more aggressive and were better pilots than we ordinarily meet. I thought perhaps these pilots were leading the rest of the attackers when they were formed up

over the fuselage. As he pulled up from overshooting the e/a, I saw the 109 pilot bale out. On our second bounce Lt. Millikan got strikes on the engine and cockpit of the e/a and he went down in a steep dive, smoking, and crashed and burned. The pilot did not get out. On the third bounce, I saw strikes all over the 109 and saw him hit the deck and burn. Things were happening so fast that I did not see this third Hun until he was hit. Lt. Millikan was doing some beautiful deflection shooting, I could see that much. After this third bounce I pulled up and found myself on Horseback's wing, so called Lt. Millikan and told him, because I knew that Lt. Norley was still my leader and at the same time, I hadn't seen Horseback's wingman so thought it best to stay with him. When Horseback went diving down after something, I was right behind him and saw Lt. Millikan firing at another 109 off my port. This e/a did a slow roll and another half-roll—that was the last I saw of them. I continued on with Horseback and came home with him. I confirm 3 Me 109s destroyed by Lt. Millikan.

and probably had the better pilots in front. Even when being attacked they tried to shoot down any of us they could. I would not have made it home had it not been for Lt. Norley's timely clobbering of one Hun, and the ready assistance of my own wingman. Every man had countless opportunities to break away and attack, but the wingmen stayed on and did their job, which is the only way the Huns Luftbery can be broken up. I claim 4 Me 109s destroyed. 666 rds. expended.

Confirmation: 2/Lt. Joseph A. Patteeuw; I was flying No. 2 to Lt. Millikan in Red section. On our first bounce I saw Lt. Millikan fire at a 109 and saw strikes all

SWEATING 'EM IN WINTER
Sergeants Tom Shiekh (radio mechanic), Charlie Brown (armourer) and Joe Kroneck (crew chief) watch their CO, Major George Bickell, let down from a grey sky on to the west runway at Boxted after a mission to Frankfurt, 29th January 1944. New 75 US gallon metal drop tanks resting on part of their wooden packing frames, made convenient perches for ground crew men.

Respect for the Supreme

The bubble canopy, six-gun P-51D reached combat squadrons of the USAAF in England during May 1944. The first examples were acquired by group and squadron commanders, for whom the enhanced view from the cockpit was a boon in keeping an eye on their own formations and the mission objective. The reaction of those transferring from the cockpit of a 'coffin hood' B or C model to the D was one of elation at the vastly improved outlook. In flight, however, the graduate soon came to complain that the D was slower in climb and level flight than its Merlin predecessors. USAAF and manufacturers' data show this to be true but the difference was minimal—about 5mph in maximum speed and a half minute on the time to 30,000 feet at maximum power—so it is surprising that this became apparent to pilots. A significant development was the D's strengthened wing allowing much heavier loads of external fuel and bombs on missions and, thus saddled, some of the temper was taken out of the Mustang. Directional control was certainly poorer due to the loss of keel area aft of the cockpit. There was, however, general approval of the increase in armament, particularly for ground strafing.

With mastery in the air the USAAF's long range escort fighters operating from England were given the go-ahead to seek out enemy airfields and shoot up his aircraft on the ground. Surprise was essential in such attacks if losses were to be minimised. Most Luftwaffe airfields were heavily defended by light anti-aircraft guns and the ideal was to strike suddenly, hard, and be away before the enemy guns could be brought to bear. Therefore it was absolutely essential to have heavy fire power so that a short well-aimed burst would be sufficient to destroy or ignite an enemy aircraft caught on the ground. The P-51B

and C with their four guns were never so effective as the Thunderbolt with its battery of eight. The P-51D with six guns went a long way to improving the work of Mustang units in this connection.

Eventually the Eighth Air Force re-equipped all but one of its 15 fighter groups with P-51Ds (and Ks), a total of 42 squadrons with, eventually, an average of 35 aircraft each. These 1,500 aircraft constituted by far and away the largest force of Mustangs operating in any theatre during World War 2 and their contribution to final victory was considerable. Between April and June 1944 two Spitfire and two Thunderbolt groups in Italy were converted to Merlin Mustangs to give them long range escort capability for heavy bombers of the US 15th Air Force. The Fifteenth's field of action was northern Italy, southern Germany and the Balkans, and while Luftwaffe fighter forces in these areas were considerably smaller than those facing the Eighth and Ninth Air Forces, the P-51s were frequently involved in combat.

While opinions were influenced by experience in flying other fighter types few, if any, USAAF pilots had anything but unfailing praise for the P-51D as a fighting machine. Colonel Jesse Thompson came to fly a variety of fighter aircraft during his Air Force career, but having entrusted his life to the Mustang during a combat tour flown with the 55th Fighter Group, it is to be expected that this aircraft ranks high in his estimation.

"I had, and have, an enormous respect for the P-51D as a combat machine. There is no doubt in my mind that, on the whole, it was the best single-seater to see action in the European theatre. I had numerous opportunities to engage in mock-combat with Spitfires over England and saw more

The second Mustang I,
AG346, taxying out at Mines
Field, Los Angeles, in the
summer of 1941. This
aircraft later saw extensive
combat service with the
RAF.

First XP-51 (41-038) procured
by the USAAF on test flight.

Left: An early P-51B on a test flight. Later served in UK.

Two of the great Mustang aces, John Godfrey and Don Gentile, who each destroyed 30 enemy aircraft. This picture was taken at Debden, England in the spring of 1944 when Godfrey (left) often flew as wingman for Gentile.

Left: Under a threatening sky A-36As are serviced at a base in the south-east United States.

D-Day at Bottisham. P-51B and Cs preparing to take off display the special black and white recognition bands used to distinguish Allied aircraft in the opening stages of the cross-channel invasion.

Two 'finger-fours' from the 375th and 376th Fighter Squadrons above a 'solid' undercast. England, July 1944.

Right: F-51D piloted by Lt. Lukakis photographed from another Mustang of the 39th Fighter Squadron in flight over Japan. Lt. Lukakis lost his life in a crash at Taegu, Korea when setting out on an operational mission.

Below: Major Herschel Green —a leading ace in the Mediterranean theatre of war with 18 air victories—in front of a 317th Fighter Squadron P-51D.

Major Sam Brown, in the cockpit of his P-51D which carries 13 victory symbols on the fuselage side. He commanded the 307th Fighter Squadron, 31st Fighter Group at San Severo, Italy.

P-51Cs of the 23rd Fighter
Group, 'Flying Tigers'
lined up on a Chinese airfield
in the summer of 1944.

A crew chief of the 332nd
Fighter Group examines skin
damage to the tail of his
P-51C caused by an exploding
shell. The negro-manned
group painted its Mustang's
tails bright red with different
coloured trim tabs to
distinguish the squadrons.
Yellow band was an aircraft
type recognition marking
used for a time in the
Mediterarean theatre.

lethal engagements with all the German fighters over the continent. I can also recall some tragic mistakes, all too common in wartime, such as an occasion when a flight of P-51s was jumped by Typhoons over Holland with fatal results for the Typhoons and another occasion when a large number of Yaks jumped a squadron of '51s over Berlin, again with fatal results for the attackers. In my opinion, the 109G was nearest to equalling the '51 in combat capability but it lacked the range and firepower of the '51. Given pilots of equal ability, which, fortunately for us, was rare, the 109 could give the '51 a real hard time.

"I respected the P-51D but cannot say I loved it. Remember, I am talking about a fully armed combat aircraft in fighting trim. I made few flights when I did not take-off with a full load of fuel and ammunition. We always took off on the main fuselage tank (right behind the cockpit) and tried to retain the remainder of that tank to come home and land on. So we always, or almost always, had a half tank of fuel to slosh around unpleasantly during combat. A pilot who had not developed techniques to allow for this could get in serious difficulties during violent manoeuvres such as occurred during low-level bombing and strafing attacks. One of the endearing qualities of the old Curtis P-40 was its unfailing habit of shaking the stick at the edge of a stall. The Mustang usually let you know that it had run out of flying speed by doing a violent snap roll—I never learned to appreciate that characteristic! On the other hand, the P-51D was easy to fly (perhaps too easy since it tended to make the novice over confident) and its comfortable ride was much appreciated during those long 7 to 7½ hour flights.

"The P-51D's best climbing angle was far less than that of the Spitfire and while the '51 could not equal the 'Spit' in level turns you could shake one by pulling into a fast diving turn. The Me 109G and the P-51D were fairly evenly matched in level manoeuvring flight but the '51 could climb and dive faster although the 109 had an advantage in initial acceleration in a dive—which often was sufficient to allow the 109 to get away. In long full power dives, the P-51D could run into compressibility with disconcerting results. Pulling out of these dives could be thrilling also . . . popped rivets (it happened to me) was the least one could expect and one pilot I knew strained his wings so much that the gear would not come down when he got home.

"The Merlin engine was a good reliable power plant. I cannot recall a single instance of primary engine failure in our group during the war. On the other hand, I never saw a Merlin that ran as smoothly as an Allison could. I never had an Allison fail on me (and I flew more hours behind the Allison) but I knew it to happen. The Merlin was hard on plugs and one always had to be changing the power setting or she could foul-up and quit on you—very embarrassing if you were very far east of the Rhine! The best plugs were British and the first thing we would do when a Packard Merlin arrived from the States was to throw away the American plugs and install the English ones.

"The Merlin P-51 had one bad habit that cost us a few pilots and a lot of sweat. The automatic air scoop door control could malfunction and drive to the fully closed position. If this happened during high-power low-level operation, the coolant temperature would rise so rapidly that, unless the pilot was really on the ball, the relief plug would blow and all the coolant would escape and 'Look Ma, no power!' This could happen in just a few minutes' time and if it took place during formation

THEY CAME BY THE HUNDRED

In the spring of 1944 large numbers of Mustangs arrived for the USAAF in both the European and Mediterranean theatres of war. A great many were unloaded from ships at Avonmouth and assembled at Filton, near Bristol, where the first job for the assembly crews was removal of a protective grease compound applied to seal out corrosive sea spray. Cockpit glassing and other sensitive areas were first protected with wax paper and oil cloth before the compound was applied. Solvent helped remove the compound but much elbow work was still required. By early April—when the photograph was taken—all P-51B and C models arriving were in natural metal finish. The P-51B in the foreground, 42-106695 was sent to the 361st Fighter Group. Above right: Photograph, taken around the same date, shows Mustangs for the Fifteenth Air Force being prepared by men of the 36th Air Depot at Maison Blanche, Algeria. The spacious hangar was inherited from the French. Red theatre nose marking and yellow type identity bands have been applied to the aircraft nearest the camera. The latter were in contrast to the white bands carried by ETO based Mustangs.

climb-out (as it usually did) the pilot's first intimation of his trouble would be a cloud of steam pouring out of the engine compartment.

"Another less endearing characteristic of the P-51D was the difficulty of baling out. Once the canopy was jettisoned the air circulation around the cockpit was such that it tended to trap the pilot *behind* the armour plate against the radio. How this came about I have never fully understood but it did happen. I'm sure level flight bale-outs were accomplished, although I never knew of one, but, so far as I was concerned the only *certain* method was from inverted flight.

"Nevertheless, despite its peculirities the P-51D was an extremely good airplane, its pilots had complete confidence in its ability to perform any reasonable mission, and its most serious detractors cannot but admit that it fulfilled its role in a superior fashion."

The role of USAAF's British based Mustangs varied considerably during the spring and summer of 1944. On one mission they would be engaged in bomber escort six miles high over Germany and on another they would be fighter-bombing an enemy ground installation in France. With the Allied invasion of the continent the number of ground attack operations increased. For these the usual load was a 500lb bomb suspended from each wing rack. It was

found that the Eighth Air Force's P-51s could be more profitably employed in patrol and strafing attacks in areas farther inland from the ground fighting. When carrying bombs the P-51 could not exploit its endurance advantage whereas the P-47 Thunderbolt with its extra shackle under the fuselage could carry drop tanks as well as ordnance ... The P-47's air-cooled radial was better suited to weathering the enemy's small arms fire in low attack, whereas a single bullet through a Mustang's coolant lines could spell disaster. P-51 losses on such missions were usually high; in fact far more were lost through strafing attacks than in air combat.

The advent of the Berger Gee-suit and the K-14 'gyroscopic' gun sight during the latter part of 1944 strengthened USAAF P-51 pilots' advantage over the enemy. The Gee suit, automatically applying pressure to the lower part of a pilot's body during very tight turns, prevented blood surge blackouts. It meant that a pilot could make tighter and safer speed turns. The K-14 gun sight was an adaptation of a British design and with simple adjustments allowed a pilot to make difficult deflection shots that would hitherto have required incredible personal skill. The Luftwaffe had rebuilt its fighter force by the autumn of that year but its new pilots were so inadequately trained that they were generally no match for the P-51 pilots. On a number of occasions when large numbers of the

enemy were encountered their air discipline was so poor that individual American pilots were able to shoot down four, five and sometimes six enemy fighters on a single mission.

A threat to the Mustang's supremacy appeared at this time, the German jet fighters. Their appearance was not unexpected if premature. The speed advantage of the most prevalent—the Me 262—was estimated at around 75 to 100mph and would undoubtedly place the Mustang and contemporary Allied fighters at a considerable disadvantage. The first British jet fighter, the Meteor, was just entering service while the US Lockheed P-80 Shooting Star could not be expected for another year. It was reasoned that the P-51 was only likely to close with an Me 262 in a dive, and then probably only with the initial advantage of surprise. It was known that fuel consumption of the jet aircraft would be very high and that it would be unlikely to have sufficient endurance to take up a favourable high altitude position to attack on-coming US formations. Attacks would most likely be launched as soon as the jet had climbed to the level of the bombers. The American force had the advantage of numbers and P-51s dispersed widely in the vicinity of the bombers should stand a fair chance of spotting Me 262s approaching and be able to make diving attacks on them. Such tactics were experimented with over England, using a

flight of the RAF's Meteors to simulate the enemy aircraft.

The Me 262 began to appear in a fighter role during October 1944 and though it undoubtedly scored many successes, Allied fighters were also able to bring down a number of the jets. In early incidents German pilots were caught off guard or mechanical difficulties gave the Allied pilots an advantage. Mustangs, foremost in these encounters, eventually improved interception techniques to bring a steady flow of victories. Many were obtained by loitering in the area of known Me 262 bases and waiting until the jets were in the vulnerable position of taking-off or landing. The speed gap between the Me 262 and the Mustang under combat conditions was not all that great and an unwary Me 262 pilot, cruising at 400 to 450mph was not a difficult quarry if the P-51 pilot had an altitude advantage.

While most jet activity involved Eighth Air Force missions, the Fifteenth's heavy bombers were occasionally intercepted by Me 262s during the final months of the war. On 24th March 1945, when the Fifteenth made its first and only raid on Berlin, a number of Me 262s attacked the B-17s but the escorting Mustangs were able to intercept many of these attacks and claimed no less than eight victories. The Negro manned 332nd Fighter Group was one of the formations involved and from an altitude vantage point dived on the jets as they came in singly or in pairs at the rear of the bomber formations. Lt. Roscoe C. Brown gave chase to one jet but lost sight of it. Looking round as he prepared to regain lost altitude he was startled to see the Me 262—or another—closing fast from behind. He instantly pushed his stick hard over and stamped on the rudder pedals to 'skid' the Mustang to one side, then taking similar action to take the aircraft in the other direction. This action apparently spoiling the German pilot's aim, causing him to overshoot and the positions were now reversed. Brown, seizing his opportunity, manoeuvred for a burst at the jet before it pulled out of range. His fire apparently hit the enemy aircraft and caused it to slow down; after a further burst the pilot baled out. Manoeuvrability was the Mustang's great advantage over the jets.

OPERATIONAL SALVAGE
The USAAF terminology for an aircraft destroyed in a crash in friendly territory. The extremely icy conditions during the first few days of 1945 brought a spate of aircraft accidents in north west Europe where freezing fog played havoc with fuel and cooling systems. On the bitter morning of 10th January 1945, P-51D 44-14480 suffered engine failure during a take-off run at Raydon. Coming off the runway onto frozen ground the right undercarriage leg failed and the engine took fire on impact. The blazing main tanks—the left drop tank was liberated and can be seen lying some distance from the aircraft—sent an ugly column of smoke into grey sky. The pilot of this aircraft escaped. Above: Not so lucky was Major James Poindexter, an experienced pilot with the same station with 7 air and 4 ground victories to his credit. The group had taken off for an escort to Aschaffenburg when Poindexter's P-51D, 44-14589, SX:G, developed a coolant leak. He turned the aircraft back towards base but the engine quickly overheated and still some five miles from Raydon, at about 1,000 feet, it seized. In an attempted belly landing in a sugar beet field the Mustang struck a tree stump in a low bank and disintegrated over the next 200 yds, killing the pilot instantly. The main fuel tanks went up in flames and ignited the ammunition preventing farm workers threshing a wheat stack (in the background) from getting near the wreckage. The spot in the village of Capel St. Mary now lies right beside the main A12 highway from Colchester to Ipswich.

The German High Command had used the first Me 262s for fast fighter-bomber operations and the first 'jet' attacks on the B-17s and B-24s were by a few Me 163 rocket-propelled fighters. Although extremely fast, capable of speeds over 600mph—these aircraft were never a serious threat due to technical troubles and their very brief endurance.

Some indication of the Me 163's performance is revealed in this account by Jesse Thompson of an incident in the Hanover-Magdeburg area:

"We were escorting B-17s at about 25,000 feet with another P-51 group above at about 30,000 feet. I saw a P-51 spinning out of control and fall through our group followed by an Me 163. I dropped my tanks, Split-S'd, balls to the wall, straight down on his tail, about 1,500 yards behind the Me 163. By the time we got down to around 10 to 12,000 feet altitude my airspeed-indicator was on the peg (beyond 575mph indicated) and I had gained to around 500 to 600 yards, still nearly vertical. Then there was a great puff of smoke from the Me 163 and he pulled away from me rapidly (and I do mean rapidly) and started to pull out of the dive. He went into an undercast at an angle of 45 to 60 degrees and about 12,000 to 15,000 yards ahead. When I broke through the clouds at about 3,000 feet he was nowhere in sight—besides I had problems of my own—the P-51 was bucking like the devil and it took both hands to get it back to level flight at around 1,500 feet. I popped a few rivets, otherwise no harm done.

Such a plunge through the atmosphere and subsequent recovery put a tremendous strain on the Mustang's airframe—far beyond the design limitations. Yet such occurrences were common in these actions to catch a jet and it is a credit to the fundamental design that the aircraft stood up to this harsh treatment. Through mishandling it was possible to put such a strain on an aircraft's components that it would break-up in the air, and some Mustangs disintegrated in such circumstances. The Mustang had been dogged by instances of structural failure, particularly since the marriage to the Merlin. Flight restrictions on dives and other manoeuvres were imposed, but in the course of combat, as related, these sometimes had to be ignored. The puzzling thing about Mustang airframe failure was that it could not be pinpointed to any one area and was sometimes encountered in brand new aircraft that had not undergone any known flight strain. Engines tore loose from fuselages, wings were shed and empenages crumpled and while most of these incidents happened during a sharp manoeuvre it was a fact that other Mustangs would engage in the same manoeuvre time and again without any sign of failure. Some components were strengthened—notably the fin and undercarriage door locks (which had a nasty habit of breaking open) but a few cases of airframe failure were regularly reported to the end of hostilities and beyond. This is not to imply that such incidents were peculiar to the Mustang : they were not.

Many early P-51Bs used by the USAAF fighter squadrons in England were retired and modified for photographic reconnaissance roles in the spring of 1944. A camera for oblique work was placed aft of the pilot's seat as on the Allison Mustangs. Many new P-51Cs were singled out for modification due to the more suitable low-altitude performance of the V-1650-7 engine (although the -3 and -7 series models were interchangeable and frequently substituted, one for the other in the field). These aircraft were used to supplement the P-51As in the Ninth Air

Force's 67th Tac. Recon. Gp., but in August 1944 that Air Force's 363rd Group changed from fighter to a tactical reconnaissance role with these camera aircraft.

Officially the designation for photographic Mustangs was F-6 but at squadron level P-51 terminology persisted. It became common for photographic Mustangs to be referred to as P-51B/F-6 or P-51C/F-6 as appropriate. The position was further complicated when these aircraft were retired from reconnaissance units and converted back to fighter configuration for use in training squadrons. Factory modifications of P-51s for camera work were leaving Dallas in the summer of 1944, chiefly as the F-6D and F-6K conversions of the P-51D and P-51K. With the cut down rear fuselage and bubble canopy on these

models it was necessary to install the camera low down in the fuselage above the radiator housing. While some modifications of this nature were effected at overseas depots it involved more engineering time so, when possible, B and C models continued to be selected for local conversions.

It was an F-6C, piloted by Lt. Robert C. Little, that is credited with shooting down the last Luftwaffe aircraft in the Second World War. At around 20.00 hours on 8th May 1945, the day hostilities officially ended, two Mustangs of the 12th Tac. Recon. Squadron were patrolling the Danube when some FW 190s appeared above them. The German pilots had either not heard that the war was over or were not inclined to lay down their arms for they immediately attempted to attack the two

Mustangs. Little reported: "My partner Lt. Fred Mitchell and I were flying above the Danube when five yellow-nosed Focke-Wulf 190s broke out of cloud about 2,000 feet above us. They attacked immediately from about 10 o'clock. All five came down together, but as they came in we banked sharply to our left so it was practically a head-on pass. Nobody fired on that first brush. They certainly weren't surrendering just then. They seemed to be out for some last minute American blood. Mitchell and I both went into a high-speed climb for position and they came right up after us. We climbed about 2,000 feet. As they followed us we peeled off and came around sharply, which put me on the tail of their last plane. My guns were right on him. I shot him down."

LAST OF THE MANY P-51C 42-103206, ZM:G flown by Lt. Robert Little of the 12th Tac. Recon. Sqn. It is believed that it was in this Mustang that Lt. Little made the last 'kill' of the Second World War in Europe.

87

Long Range Escort

On most of the large heavy bomber missions flown by the Eighth Air Force during the last six months of the war, a force of over seven hundred Mustangs accompanied the B-17s and B-24s. One of the fourteen fighter groups operating from England was the 353rd which adorned its aircraft with yellow and black striped spinners and checkerboard noses. Based at Raydon, near Ipswich, the group's three squadrons had about one hundred Mustangs on hand during this period, mostly P-51Ds and some Ks for operations, plus a few P-51B and C models for training purposes. During the latter stages of hostilities most escort missions were uneventful in respect of contact with enemy aircraft. For the onlooker the sheer spectacle of the despatch and return of one of these missions never lost its appeal.

READY ROOM
Above left: Pilots of 352nd Fighter Squadron await a call to briefing. A tense period when some tried to read or write letters, while others just lounged.

SEARS ROEBUCK IF THE MISSION'S ABANDONED
Left: Information display boards in the briefing room give the various code words to use in radio communication, weather details, flare colours and check-point times. Courses of the main bomber and fighter formations are plotted on the wall map, the broad lower ribbon being that for the 353rd Group. The mission will last four hours and take the group's Mustangs 350 miles to meet the bombers over Germany.

ROLL!
Right: Seats down, canopies closed, 350th FS Mustangs on the main runway. Pilots not assigned to fly on a mission often acted as marshalls at take-off. To hasten assembly of a formation aircraft took off in pairs, the wingman slightly behind his leader. As each pair lifted off the next commenced its run. The Mustang's nose prevented pilots from seeing when the pair ahead left the ground. Marshallers positioned themselves in the pilot's view and waved off each pair. A draughty job in the blast from Merlins under power.

PILOTS ARRIVE
Left: Lt. F. Stapp and Lt. W. Manahan indulge in a little hangar flying before they climb into their aircraft. Personal equipment includes helmet with built-in ear-phones and attached plug-in radio cables, 'Mae West' life saver and oxygen mask and supply tube.

READY AND WAITING
Below: 'Double Trouble', with witch and warrior-duck motifs, waits for its pilot, Lt. Col. Bill Bailey, commander of 352nd Fighter Squadron. Tyres are depressed by the weight of a full load of fuel (485 US gallons) and ammunition (1,880 rounds) adding approximately 5,500 lb to the P-51D's empty basic weight of 7,150 lb. This aircraft, officially 44-14303; SX:B, has a K-25 camera fixed to the back of the pilot's head-rest for oblique photography. Despite the excellent view from the P-51's cockpit, many pilots still liked to have a rear-view mirror for quick 'clear-my-tail' checks. Location varied according to personal preference.

69

MISS ELLEN DIDN'T MAKE IT

Above: Engine trouble at lift-off was every pilot's dread. P-51D, 44-15671, LH:P quit just as the gear was coming up and careered away from one side of the runway ending up in a pile of empty 108 gallon drop tanks still clutching two full ones. Miraculously there was no fire. Airfield vehicles rushing to the spot carry yellow flags on tall masts. These were an aid to help taxying Pilots spot vehicles.

CLIMBING OUT

Above: The 351st Fighter Squadron orbits the base area gaining altitude over the Suffolk countryside. Close finger-fours, echeloned down from the lead flight so that there was no excuse for losing the formation, gave place to widely spaced, line abreast battle flights once hostile airspace was reached. In this photograph no drop tanks are being carried indicating a short duration mission.

THEY SURE GOT CLOBBERED

Left: Thirty thousand feet above Germany fighter pilots often had a good view of the bombing—and the awesome flak barrages the bombers met at the target. Here smoke rises thousands of feet into the air from a target the heavy bombers have just left. Traces of marker bomb smoke plumes can still be seen crinkling in the sky. A seat-rest mounted camera in a 351st FS element leader's Mustang took this picture, catching the wingman flying battle position 600 yards away.

FORMING UP

Below: 'Betty E', 44-72374, LH:U, personal mount of Lt. Col. Wayne Blickenstaff, gaining altitude after take-off. Once airborne the leading element executed a wide left-hand turn, orbiting the base while other elements and sections of the squadron joined them. A 16-plane squadron would be airborne in four minutes and a three-squadron group of 48 in 13 minutes.

RENDEZVOUS WITH BIG FRIENDS

Below left: Flying some 3,000 feet above the bombers the group takes over escort. One squadron is split each side of the bomber formation, another flies a mile ahead and the third 10 miles ahead up sun. Depending on the particular requirements of the Field Order, escort groups would shepherd their assigned bombers for specified periods, taking-over from and being relieved by other fighter groups. On a 'solid undercast' the straight shadows of bomber contrails and the curving and crossing ones of escort fighters would often be visible to enemy interceptors long before they could see their quarry and its protectors.

AN INDIVIDUAL TOUCH

Bottom: Captain William Tanner's Mustang was unusual for the 353rd Group in having part of the upper surfaces painted with dark green. This was to make the aircraft less conspicuous from above when ground strafing and so lessen the chance of being 'jumped' by enemy interceptors. When camouflage paint was deleted from factory production it was estimated that the reduced drag and weight added an extra 5 mph to top speed. In practice, paint did not appear to make all that much difference, although precise assessment was difficult due to individual variations in top speed between aircraft with identical specifications. In any case, the use of wax or Fullers Earth to polish aircraft became common in some units and this did aid performance by giving smoother air flow. (Note the shine on the painted surface of 'Prudence 7th's wing).

Clean, and with half combat fuel load, a P-51D could top 430 mph in level flight.

HOLDING OFF

Below: The tail begins to come down as Captain Dewey Newhart prepares to put 'Arkansas Traveler II' down on the hard. A Mustang was best 'flown into' a landing and treated firmly. Two mirrors, one attached to each side of the windshield frame, were preferred by this pilot.

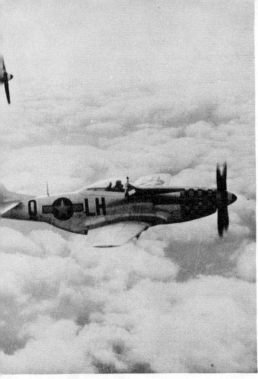

HOMEWARD BOUND
Above left: Closed up and devoid of drop tanks a flight of 350th FS Mustangs head home over the clouds. VHF homings brought these fighters safely back over the then incredible distances of five to six hundred miles. Special relay aircraft flying off the enemy coast extended radio coverage on long missions. P-51Ds in the photograph are Lt. L. W. Lee's 414690,LH:Q, Lt. Manahan's 'Lady Gwen II' 44-15589,LH:G, and 44-14111, LH:Q.

COMING IN
Above: Flaps down, propeller control forward to 2,700 rpm, 110 IAS over the threshold: a 351st Ftr. Sqn. aircraft homes in on the south-east runway as three other Mustangs prepare to break formation. The black and white checkered control wagon sports a Fortress nosepiece over the observation hatch.

MISSION COMPLETED
Left: While a Fortress group heads for its base in Essex, a flight of Mustangs 'peel-off' over No 1 hangar at Raydon to make their landing approaches. Raydon was built as a bomber field with hard surfaced runways and aircraft standings but being surplus to bomber requirements always housed fighter units.

95

Give and Take

Battle Damage

RIGHT IN D'ASS
Above: The 364th Fighter
Group's 44-14254:5E:G, took
a direct hit from a 40 mm
shell during a strafing raid
on 24th October 1944.
Despite a jammed rudder
the pilot brought the
aircraft back to Honington.
POLE FELLER
Below: The result of
unintentional destruction
of part of the enemy's
telephone system near Ulm
on 17th February 1945.

Capt. Bob Maloney, 55th
Fighter Group, was engaged
in attacking a train when
this happened to
44-15421, CG:Z.
**YE GODS, WHAT YOU BIN
DOIN' TO MY PLANE?**
Above right: A favourite
quip with crew chiefs and
applicable to this scene. Lt.
Louis DeAnda and S/Sgt
James Tolleson of the 78th
Fighter Group examine a
hole made by a 20 mm shell
in WZ:T while DeAnda was
strafing a train in Germany
on 23rd February 1945.

VERY NEAR MISS
Right: Lt. Millard Anderson
shows fellow 55th Fighter
Group pilot Capt. Donald
Penn tears caused by shell
fragments while strafing an
enemy airfield.
Both pilots are wearing late
type goggles. These had
replaceable panels and were
tinted to cut down sun glare.
They were also worn to
protect the eyes against
flash burn, oil or coolant
in the event of the aircraft
being badly hit.

Faces of the Aces

In the last year of hostilities in Europe many Mustang pilots flew a complete combat tour—about 200 hours —without ever engaging in air combat. The dominant Allied air forces could then field over 8,000 fighters and there were fewer opportunities for individuals to reach ace status. An ace was the unofficial accolade for a fighter pilot who had brought down five or more opponents. Few pilots ran their scores into double figures during this period, but there were notable exceptions.

RAY WETMORE
Right: Those deep-set slits of eyes were deceptive. Time and again he would spot distant enemy aircraft that fellow members of his group, the 359th, did not or could not see. 'Old X-ray Eyes' they called him as the number of swastikas painted on the side of his green-nosed Mustang 'Daddy's Girl' grew to over twenty. A total of 170 pilots served with the 359th Group's three squadrons but only one other ace had air victories in double figures (10½) giving some indication of how outstanding was Wetmore's record. The PRO boys posed this photo after a dog fight in which the 22 year old pilot claimed four victories.

BILL, CLAUDE & RATSY
Below: A great many of the German fighters encountered during the summer of 1944 were flown by pilots with insufficient training. These were shot out of the sky in large numbers when they challenged the experienced American escort. On one such occasion, 21st November, Capt. William Whisner (left) knocked down six FW 190s and Lt. Claude Crenshaw (right) five. With them (centre) is George Preddy, who destroyed a single FW 190 on the same mission to bring his total of victories to 25½. He also had destroyed 6 enemy aircraft during a mission. Preddy, killed by 'friendly' flak on the following Christmas Day, was the highest scoring Mustang ace of the war (24 in Mustangs).

CHUCK YEAGER
Above: Yet another man who made several kills on one mission was Lt. Charles Yeager of the 357th Group. Leading the group formation on 12th October 1944, he was involved in a dog-fight and was credited with five Me 109s destroyed. Here Corporal Jay Bingaman paints the symbols for these victories on 'Glamorous Glen II'. Yeager was shot down earlier in the year over France but evaded capture. In later years he would become famous as the first man to exceed the speed of sound in level flight while flying the Bell X-1 experimental jet.

JET JUMPER
Left: Downing an Me 262 jet was a great achievement— it was 100mph faster than the mustang. Urban Drew went one better. On 7th October 1944, while flying at 15,000 feet over Achmer airfield in north Germany, he saw two unidentified aircraft taking off. He put his Mustang, 'Detroit Miss' 44-14164, E9:D, into a 450 mph dive and was gaining on the last aircraft to leave the runway when he realised it was a jet. A short burst of fire hit its target and then, as the speed of his dive caused him to overshoot Drew lined up on the leading Messerschmitt and clobbered that. When he looked back both aircraft had crashed and exploded.

MUSTANG NEEDS MAN: MAN NEEDS GOD
Right: Using his jeep as an improvised altar and with the aid of a miniature organ, the Protestant chaplain of the 339th Fighter Group leads ground crews in singing Easter hymns at chill Fowlmere. Behind stands 'Happy IV' (44-64148, 5Q:C), personal mount of C.O., Col. William Clarke.

Keeping 'em flying

CONTINENTAL COMFORTS
Centre left: Servicing a
Mustang in the open was
often a miserable job.
Lashed by rain and bitter
winter winds the ground
crew's lot was unenviable.
Hangar shelter was limited
and in the UK only available
for major repair. When the
352nd Fighter Group was
moved to Chierves, Belgium
early in 1945, they were able
to make use of the aircraft
shelters the Luftwaffe had
erected and disguised as
farm houses and buildings.
'We Three', (44-13533;PE:U)
and 'Oklahoma Kid' receive
attention outside one of these
shelters, while within its
dark interior sits another
Mustang.
CAN I GIVE YOU A SHINE?
Left: A crew chief's pride is
reflected by this P-5IC.
S/Sgt Bill Accoo, 99th FS,
washes the waxed surface
with soap and water. Waxing
helped smooth the air flow
and added more speed.

WITH CARE
Above: In summer the
elements were kinder,
particularly down in Italy
where the only all-Negro
manned fighter group in the
USAAF was based. This was
the 332nd, one of the four
Mustang groups assigned to
the 15th Air Force. Its
mechanics established a very
high serviceability record for
their aircraft. A crew chief
fussed around his plane as
if it were a life's investment.
S/Sgt Alfred Morris main-
tained the P-51C flown by
100th Fighter Squadron
operations Officer Captain
Bill Mattison. Like all crew
chiefs he would be the last
man up on the wing to close
the canopy after discussing
how 'she sings' with the pilot.

PICKABACK
Below: A non-text book way of trying to solve a technical difficulty at Raydon. When a vibration problem was found in a P-51K, Major Rose, the Air Inspector, and Mr. Slyter, technical representative of the makers, went aloft in this fashion, Major Rose uncomfortably doubled up under the canopy.

Above: Absolute cleanliness was essential if guns were to work without jamming. Armourers disassembled, cleaned, checked and lubricated the Point Fifties after every action. The gun weighed 65 lb and fired 800 rounds per minute with a muzzle velocity of 2,900 feet per second. This gave it much greater hitting power and range than the smaller 0.30 machine guns used by many air forces.

INGENUITY
Right: Many of the modifications embodied in the Mustang originally stemmed from the ideas of ground crew men. The preferred installation of the K-14 'gyro' gunsight was based on the pioneer work of an Eighth Air Force mechanic. Some of the first sights— which allowed pilots to engage in accurate deflection shooting—were allocated to the 357th Fighter Group at Leiston. It was found that they could not be safely installed in the P-51D without considerable modification. A member of the armament section designed and constructed a special recessed mount, the first example (shown here) on the CO's personal aircraft 'Bodacious'.

Expendable Appendages

BOMBS

Left/Below: The two under-wing racks on late production Mustangs were designed to carry a maximum load of 1,000 lb each. Normal HE 500 or 1,000 lb bombs were the general load for ground attack but practically every type of weapon within the weight limitations of the fighter was tried operationally. The cumbersome looking cluster attached to the rack of Captain J. W. Edwards' Mustang is made up of 12 × 30 lb anti-personnel fragmentation bombs, nasty weapons designed to mow down enemy troops with flying fragments. A rare one was the parachute bomb, designed to obtain greater blast effect and lessen penetration, the device was suspended by three small parachutes after release.

PICTURE PACKIN' GENERAL

Left: The 353rd Fighter Group devised a highly successful mount, attached to the rear of the pilot's armour plate, for holding a K-24 camera. With this pilots were able to take excellent oblique photographs of ground targets they had strafed. Commander of the Eighth Air Force's 3rd Air Division, Major General Earle Partridge, heard about this and flew his personal Mustang down to Raydon to have a fitting. With this camera the General took photographs of badly spaced bomber formations assembling for missions and used this evidence to educate formation leaders.

YANK TANK
Left: A few shipments of the US made 110 gallon metal tank were received in the UK in the summer of 1944 but for the most part this type of tank was used by Italian based units and those in Japanese war zones. The first installation of one of these tanks at Honington is illustrated here as mechanics make final adjustments to the 'plumbing'. Short pieces of glass tubing in this system ensured clean breaks when the tanks were released. The exhaust from the aircraft's instrument vacuum pump provided pressurisation for these tanks, a necessity if fuel was to be drawn successfully at high altitudes.

BABIES
Above: Drop tanks were the most common attachment on racks of Eighth, Ninth and Fifteenth Air Force Mustangs. With two of these it was possible for a Mustang to stay aloft for more than nine hours although this was beyond reasonable endurance expected of any pilot. The longest escort missions were of seven or eight hours. The most popular type of tank was the 108 US gallon 'paper' type manufactured by the Bowater organisation in the UK. Plastic/pressed paper composition made it extremely light as WO Cecil Broxton demonstrates here. With two of these the combat range—allowing for the usual type of escort/bomber support mission undertaken by the Eighth Air Force— was more than double that on internal fuel alone. 'Baby' was the code name for a drop tank.

104

Bent and Broken

NOSED

Left: M/Sgt Roy Lineberry examines the extent of damage to the reduction gear case on this white-nosed 355th Fighter Group P-51D. The aircraft was bellied in on a French field after the engine siezed through overheating. A single rifle calibre bullet penetrating a coolant line was the cause of its demise. Abrasive action of the soil has removed the paint from a large part of the buckled propeller blades.

BIG SMOKE

Left: This Mustang may look in trouble but it is actually laying a smoke screen from chemical tanks attached to the bomb racks. The tanks were designed for smoke, or gas dispensing but were rarely used in combat. This particular display was carried out over Kingscliffe airfield by Maj. M. Gilbertson in 'Sad Sack', purely for educational or 'just for the hell of it' purposes.

TAILED

Above/Above left: War Weary 43-6928,CY:9 has two empennages, its own and that of 'Skippy' (P-51D 44-13743) tucked under its nose. All as a result of a pilot not seeing what was ahead on the perimeter track at Wormingford one pleasant April afternoon in 1945. The War Weary is an aircraft operated by the station's operational training unit and

was modified to carry a passenger in the section aft of the pilot's seat—normally occupied by the radio and auxiliary fuel tank. Most Mustang groups in Europe had one of these two-seat adaptions, and all were individually tailored. As the aircraft's C of G was affected, aerobatics were forbidden in these twosomes.

BITING THE DUST
Right: Coming in to land at Bad Abling, Germany a few days after the end of hostilities, a 22nd Tac. Recon. Sqn F-6D was involved in a spectacular crash in full view of a POW compound. The right wingtip caught the wreck of an Me 109 and cartwheeled the Mustang round, completely wrecking it. The Mustang pilot escaped with a few minor cuts and bruises.

CANNIBALISED
Right: All useful useable parts were stripped from this 385th Fighter Squadron P-51D, (44-15726:5E:X) before it was carted away for salvage. An engine failure on take-off caused the pilot to crash-land on a ploughed field near his Honington base. Damage was too great for economical repair and by this date—April 1945—there was no shortage of new aircraft.

ALL DOLLED UP
The markings on USAAF aircraft in combat squadrons were, to say the least, extensive. This Mustang with a perplexing variety was operated by the Operational Training Unit of the 55th Fighter Squadron, 20th Fighter Group. The tail number, 2106476, was the official USAAF 'radio-call number' for communication purposes, a slightly abbreviated form of the serial number, the overall individual identity marking. The letters LC were code for the 55th Fighter Squadron and carried by all Mustangs of that unit. 'Zee-Bar' was the individual aircraft identity within the squadron and as there were more than 26 aircraft assigned duplicated individual letters were distinguished by a bar painted beneath them. The black circular background to the Zee-Bar on the fin and rudder is additional squadron marking within the group—the other two squadrons used a triangle and a square. The letters WW stand for War Weary and indicate the aircraft is subject to flight restrictions because of the large number of flying hours it has seen. The black nose stripes are the identification markings of the 20th Fighter Group and the all black spinner identifies an OTU aircraft whereas combat P-51s of the group had part black, part white spinners.

Improving the Breed

The basic design of the Mustang, structurally and aerodynamically, was so good that its development to meet the ever advancing performance requirements of the military always proceeded apace and was never fraught with any great difficulties. Following the advent of the Merlin P-51B and C models only one other major production development would come to play a part in the Second World War. This was the P-51D of which 7,956 were completed together with 1,337 P-51Ks which were practically identical apart from a propeller change. These amounted to by far the largest number of a Mustang type—approaching two thirds of all aircraft contracted as P-51s.

The distinguishing feature of this development evolved from an early P-51B extensively modified to incorporate a 360% vision cockpit canopy. Advanced manufacturing techniques enabled such transparent pieces to be durable enough to withstand the great variations in temperature and stresses normal in fighter operations. Many British and German interceptors had these all-round vision canopies and the excellent view they afforded pilots helped greatly in reducing fatigue. Towards the end of 1943 criticisms of the P-51B's firepower induced North American to increase armament from four to six wing guns and improve ammunition stowage. At the same time the wing was to be strengthened to take heavier loads on the external bomb and tank racks. Two P-51Bs were thus modified in December 1943, incorporating also the 360% vision canopy and other minor refinements. These were redesignated as P-51Ds and although prototypes, they were not identified with the usual X prefix as they stemmed from a manufacturer initiated project and were not specially funded. The D superseded the B model on the Inglewood production lines

in February 1944 and at Dallas in July that year.

The P-51D with its additional armament was heavier than the preceding models by about 450lb. While this was not a great jump it did have a noticeable effect on performance and North American engineers were also conscious that half a ton had been added to the Mustang since the first Allison models flew in 1941. The mounting weight problem bedevilled all aircraft development projects. Despite its good showing the Mustang was now nearly 2,000lb heavier than some Spitfire models and by comparison lacked acceleration and had a relatively poor rate of climb. But long before the P-51D was in production a thorough reappraisal of the basic design with a view to saving weight was put in hand. As a start it was felt that much could be learned from a study of British load factor technique and in the spring of 1943 Edgar Schmued and a party from North American went to the UK for this purpose. As a result of information gathered and the Company's own ideas, a design proposal for a light-weight Mustang was approved by the USAAF and a contract for prototypes followed in July 1943. Three of these with the current Packard Merlin V-1650-3 engines were designated XP-51F while two others, designated XP-51G, were to have a new engine from Rolls-Royce, the Merlin 100, which would be shipped from the UK as soon as available. One XP-51F and one XP-51G were requested by the British for evaluation in the UK.

The aim of the preliminary design study on the lightweight Mustangs was to save some 1,300lb. Where possible the original structure was simplified, some items were deleted, smaller and lighter components obtained and new materials and processes of construction used. The re-design of the wing involved proportionately thinner aerofoil to give less drag, and the ironing out of the leading edge kink (as viewed in plan form) by using smaller wheel, brake and undercarriage leg assemblies. Armament was reduced to four 'point fifties'. Further weight was saved by deleting the fuselage fuel tank and the oil cooling core in the radiator, the latter being replaced by a heat exchanger situated in the engine compartment. A three-blade Aeroproducts propeller with broad hollow blades saved several pounds over the four-blade Hamilton gear. All told, the first XP-51F, which made its maiden flight on 14th February, 1944, grossed 7,610lb with normal load, as against 10,100lb for the D model and 9,200lb for the B. Top speed in level flight proved to be 30 miles per hour faster than the D and the XP-51F could reach 20,000 ft 2.3 minutes faster than the D.

The two other XP-51Fs were ready for flight in May 1944 and subsequently one of these was shipped to England at the end of June. The first XP-51G did not fly until 9th August for although the Merlin 100 engines had arrived from Rolls-Royce in February, the novel fuel injection apparatus posed air mixture problems that necessitated some experimentation and modification work to the associated components. This prototype gave a superlative performance scaling 20,000ft of altitude in only 3.4 minutes and then speeded along at 485mph—the RAF even extracted an additional ten miles per hour from the second XP-51G on trials at Boscombe Down in February 1945. But both the XP-51F and G were far from perfect and had distinct vices; in particular, heavy rudder forces and lack of direction stability in some flight attitudes. While the XP-51G offered exceptional advances in performance the Merlin 100 was not in full production so the first contract for the light-weight Mustang, approved on 30th June 1944, was for 2,400 P-51Hs, refined versions of the XP-51F.

When it appeared in February 1945 the P-51H had an upgraded Packard Merlin, the V-1650-9, fitted with water injection and an auto-boost control device. A P-51D type canopy took the place of the longer, more streamlined type, installed on XP-51F and XP-51G, and a dorsal extension was fitted to the fin to aid directional stability. However, after the first 20 aircraft, all P-51Hs featured an enlarged fin and rudder to further improve stability. Otherwise the P-51H was similar to the experimental lightweights and had a comparable top speed, but being somewhat heavier lagged in climb performance—although appreciably better than the earlier Merlin Mustangs. Two further lightweight P-51 prototypes were constructed in 1944 to take the experimental Allison V-1710-119 engine, featuring water injection as a means towards extracting 1,720hp at around 20,000 feet. Engine problems saw the XP-51Js—as these were designated—passed to Allison for experimental trials. The first flew in April 1945, while the second is said to have been utilised as spares for the first. Although performance was good, at this late date the aircraft could not be a serious contender for war production.

The P-51K was a Dallas factory model which was simply a D with a different type of propeller. Such was the rate of P-51 production in the spring of 1944 that the situation was foreseen when insufficient Hamilton Standard propellers would be forthcoming to meet the needs of both factories. Consequently plans were made to use a propeller from another manufacturer. This was Aeroproducts', featuring hollow steel blades and a faster actuating mechanism for blade angle change. As it was some

90lb lighter than the Hamilton, it was considered that the change would be advantageous to aircraft performance. However, it was soon found that many P-51Ks vibrated badly due to faulty propeller balance. Vibration was not apparent with every Aeroproducts airscrew but a great deal of changing had to be undertaken with consequential delays in delivery of aircraft. After making 1,500 Ks the factory reverted to P-51Ds.

P-51L was the designation given to an improved version of the P-51H intended to feature the V-1650-11 Merlin but this never materialised due to the cessation of hostilities and cancelled orders. The Dallas plant was to have produced the P-51M, similar to the D but using the same engine as the P-51H, less water injection. The single example built was the last P-51 produced by that plant when production ended in September 1945. P-51H production at Inglewood finished in November 1945. The only Mustang variant still in production was the P-82 Twin Mustang, an ingenious design to meet the exigencies of the Pacific campaign where very long overwater flights taxed the stamina of both pilot and aircraft. In simple terms, Mustang airframes were coupled; although the P-82 actually featured enough new or redesigned components to make it a completely different aircraft as a production proposition. Two lengthened fuselages of the lightweight Mustang type, connected by a wing and tail section both of constant chord, had outer wing panels also similar to the lightweight Mustang design. Each of the new heavier main undercarriage assemblies was positioned beneath the outer wing roots to retract inwards under the fuselage and centre wing section. Opposite rotating propellers were fitted to the Merlins of the first XP-82, appearing in April 1945, but the following prototypes used the water injection Allisons as experimentally tested in the XP-51J.

There were a great many experimental versions of production Mustangs, testing new equipment or improved features, both sides of the Atlantic. British agencies experimented with various weapon loads, and engine modifications, and ran trials to assess its suitability for varying roles. In November 1944 the US Navy carried out successful deck landing trials on the carrier *Shangri-La* with a P-51D fitted with an arrester hook. But, for the most part, the experimental Mustangs had no significant influence on the aircraft reaching combat squadrons during the final eighteen months of the Second World War. It was the B, C, D, and K models that were flown in combat and whatever their shortcomings in the light of later developments, they were well equal to the task—and considerably superior in all round performance to most Allied or enemy fighter types.

On the Line in England

Merle Olmsted

Hardly any of our group had been in the UK before, so everything, the people, cars, food, trains, beer—and the weather, were all new to us. The blackout, and the way the natives got around it, stand out in my memory. We had difficulty understanding the people at first (and they us) and the money was a problem, but both of these soon smoothed out.

We found the weather unpleasant, but then, it had been unpleasant most everywhere we had been, so it was nothing new. I remember the standing joke about it though—if one should chance to oversleep some morning, he might well miss summer!

We began getting our P-51s (all B Models) while at Raydon Wood, and all were hand-downs, either from the RAF, or the 354th Fighter Group, which had preceded us with the type. The Mustang was completely strange to all, air and ground crews. As far as I know, no one had had any training on them, although later many went off to various P-51 related schools, such as the RAF Merlin engine school which I attended.

Even though the P-51 was a strange bird to us, I think we all knew that we had a winner, and we had never felt that way about the Bell P-39. As for major maintenance problems, looking back I don't think we had any! Compared to the incredibly sophisticated fighters of the sixties and seventies, the P-51 was primitive, but that certainly paid off from the maintenance point of view. Even so, I think the P-51 was more trouble-free than other fighters of the period, such as the P-47. Coolant leaks were a common, but minor problem. A puddle under the aircraft was often found in the mornings, but putting a fingertip in the liquid and touching it to the tongue soon indicated whether it was coolant—which had a very bitter taste.

Spark plugs, and the resulting rough engine, were a constant headache. British plugs, which were the best, would only give about 15 hours' operating time. The exhaust plugs were easy to change of course, but the intake plugs were tricky to change in a hot engine, as they always were, it seems, and plugs that were dropped between the intake manifolds usually stayed there, as they were impossible to retrieve. I would like to see the figures on our plug consumption, we must have used literally thousands of them.

Engine change time on a P-51 was 200 hours but not many made it that far under strenuous combat conditions. After we went to 150 grade fuel we had a lot of

valve trouble which cut engine life. Still the Merlin was one hell of a fine engine.

The start of a line crew's day depended entirely on the scheduled briefing time for the pilots. If the weather was 'dud' we slept late: Crews were usually breakfasted and on the line before daylight or soon after, again depending on briefing time.

We were fortunate with the P-51 in that they were not maintenance hogs and we usually had our work finished by evening chow time. This doesn't mean that we never worked on into the night—we did, but not often enough to gripe about! The hangar crew (which did engine changes and other heavy maintenance) usually had a separate night shift.

Living quarters were a mile or two from the airfield, most of the fields built for the Americans were this way. Transport was via hitching a ride on a truck, jeep, or weapons carrier. A quantity of RAF cycles were issued, and other people bought their own, but failing that then one walked! Most crews built a shack near their hardstand, constructed from belly tank boxes. Some were quite plush with windows, workbenches and bunks. A few had stoves, burning used engine oil, but this was a hazardous method of obtaining warmth and after a few shacks went up like fire bombs, Eighth Air Force put a stop to it.

In our squadron, three men made up the ground crew on one aircraft. In the case of

Crew Chief Staff Sergeant Ray Morrison (left) and his assistant Sergeant Merle Olmsted pause from their labours for another crewman and his camera. Olmsted is holding a spray gun with its hose running down an ammunition can filled with gasoline. A standard practice amongst Eighth Air Force mechanics at the time, this method of cleaning would be viewed with horror in later more safety conscious days. The Mustang is P-51D, 44-72489, G4:P, nicknamed 'Rolla U'—name of the pilot's girlfriend plus a ranch brand mark. In the background can be seen one of the hardstand shacks made from packing cases with a corrugated iron roof.

our crew we were together from assignment in the States till the end of the war. The crew chiefs picked were usually the 'older' men in their 20s, or the very elderly—in their 30s. I was just a youngster, 19, and was assigned as Assistant Crew Chief. The assistant C/C also filled in with other aircraft in the flight when those Mustangs were without crews (leave, illness or other duty). The third man was armament of course. Whoever arrived first in the morning (C/C or Asst. C/C) started the preflight. The armament man usually arrived much later, as he had checked his guns and loaded his ammo cans after the previous day's mission. About all he had to do was make another quick check of the solenoids and firing circuits, and charge the guns. Most aircraft had nicknames,

these were usually, but not always, chosen by the pilot. Colonel Dregne, the group commander, had two names on his P-51 (as did a few others), his choice on one side and the crew chief's on the other. Sometimes the name was painted on by the pilot and sometimes by the crew—I painted several myself. Some of the more elaborate ones in my squadron, such as Roberson's 'Passion Wagon', and Weager's beautiful nude, were done by a talented crew chief.

During the fourteen months my squaddron, the 362nd, was on combat status, our crew received five aircraft. We were lucky in that we only lost two and then not through enemy action. The first two were early B models and were replaced for technical reasons. Then we had a late B nicknamed 'Joan' by its first pilot and, after he'd finished his tour, 'Floogie' by Lt. 'Dittie' Jenkins, who took over the plane. Jenkins had to belly 'Floogie' in near Brussels in October 1944 after the engine threw a rod. The replacement was a P-51D which Jenkins named 'Floogie II'. Another pilot, Lt. Schleiker was killed in this aircraft in January 1945 when it disintegrated during a mission due to some unknown failure. Lt. Ed Hyman flew our last charge, 'Rolla U', a late production D and it was still going strong at the end of the war. Of course, some crews lost pilots in combat and got through a lot more aircraft.

The relationship between pilots and crews was good. There were a few pilots the enlisted men did not like, and there were a few pilots who treated the ground crews as inferior beings, but these were a very small percentage, and in general we were a happy family. I do know that the pilots who were associated with our crew got along fine, and one of them, Ed Hyman, the last assigned pilot of our P-51, occasionally used to join me in trips to London.

We Just Didn't Suit

Diana Hutchinson Smith

An American ace tells the story of the day he became aware that he was doing nothing clever in piloting a Mustang. He was preparing to leave an RAF airfield after refueling when a Mustang with British markings executed a copy-book landing approach and three-point touch down. When the aircraft taxied in and parked beside his own Mustang he was astonished to see a slim girl climb out of the cockpit.

Many men were similarly enlightened that flying military aircraft was not a male prerogative. While the fair sex were restricted to the non-combat task of ferrying, it could be a hazardous occupation in the face of poor weather or when an aircraft developed mechanical troubles. Women in Air Transport Auxiliary (ATA) coped with emergencies as efficiently as the men. Third Officer Miss M. Shiel was given a commendation for her handling of a difficult situation in a Mustang I. On the afternoon of 24th February 1945, soon after take-off on a delivery flight, the engine started to splutter and shortly thereafter cut out completely—it was subsequently established that a main bearing had failed. With considerable skill Miss Shiel managed to make a safe wheels-up landing in a small field near Barry (South Wales). This aircraft, AG362, was the eighteenth Mustang made.

In contrast to the laudatory comments of most pilots who flew the Mustang, one of the most experienced ferry pilots, First Officer Diana Hutchinson Smith considered it the only aircraft she disliked of all the 56 different types she flew in three years with ATA. In delivering many hundreds of aircraft she never bent or broke one but came very close to it with the Mustang on several occasions.

The Mustang was definitely the aircraft that gave me the most uncomfortable moments of my time with ATA. I disliked it intensely. Admittedly it was a purely personal thing, we just didn't suit each other. Three times I nearly dropped one from a great height during landing approaches.

The first occasion was in February 1945 on a flight from Silloth (near Carlisle) to Cosford, our No. 12 Ferry Pool. While making my approach the aircraft suddenly dropped, apparently in a down-draught, a nasty sensation. The following month I was delivering a Mustang IV from 38 MU at Llandow to 12 FU at Melton Mowbray when quite unexpectedly the same sort of thing happened but fortunately it didn't quite stall.

While admitting that my experience in the Mustang was limited—I don't suppose I flew more than a dozen—one thoroughly studied the White Book (The ATA Technical Handling Notes) so as to be aware of any flight peculiarities. In retrospect, I think I was unfortunate enough to run into down-draughts on these occasions. However, the third time was a very near thing. It was undoubtedly due to a strong down-draught at a critical moment.

It happened on 12th April when I took another Mustang IV (KM304) from Cosford to the Rootes modification plant at Meir, near Stoke-on-Trent, a small aerodrome having a rather short runway which was approached over a built-up area. While letting down the aircraft nearly stalled over houses but fortunately we arrived in one piece.

As it happened, I was never asked to ferry another Mustang. The last experience made a lasting impression—probably most unfairly—but for me it was a horrible aeroplane.

Guns and Ammo

Leroy Nitschke

An armourer's lot was more than loading the hardware for a Mustang to deliver to the enemy. It involved constant sessions of cleaning and inspection to ensure that delivery could be made. There was nothing more frustrating for a pilot with an enemy lined up in the sight than to have his guns fail when the firing button was squeezed. A situation an armourer dreaded happening to the weapons he maintained and one he did his utmost to see would not occur. M/Sgt. Leroy Nitschka, 'Ole Nick' to his friends, looked after the guns in Mustangs of the 334th Fighter Squadron at Debden, England. This was a unit of the 4th Fighter Group, direct descendant of the RAF's three 'Eagle Squadrons'. Some of the RAF's slang persisted at Debden as Nitschke's account of an armourer's work reveals.

After each show the guns were checked to see if they had been fired and if so they were removed from the bays and taken to the armament shack for cleaning and a thorough inspection. All working parts had to be carefully examined for wear or damage. Occasionally gun barrels were found to be warped. This happened when a pilot fired a very long burst and the barrels overheated.

Ammunition had to be changed or additional rounds added to each belt to build up the required amount. Usually if more than 25 rounds had been fired the ammunition was changed to avoid combining two issued lots—all belted lengths supplied by the ammo dump were carefully documented with lot numbers. The feed trays of a P-51B held a maximum of 1,260 rounds, the inboard guns having 350 rounds each and the outer guns 280. On the P-51D with its six 'point fifties' the total was increased to 1,880 with the inboard having 400 rounds each and the

two outer weapons 270 apiece. An aircraft seeing a lot of action on a mission would frequently only have rounds left for the two inner guns when it returned. In practice, the number of rounds made available for each gun in a P-51 varied from base to base depending on the individual requirement of a particular group. However, it was general with all units to place five rounds of incendiary before the last 25 in a belt to warn the pilot he was running low.

All ammunition drawn from the squadron dump—even if new—was run through a repositioning machine to ensure that it would be correctly positioned in the metal clip belts. Many gun malfunctions were due to ammo being improperly aligned. Dirt or grease was another cause of trouble and ammunition returned to the dump had to be cleaned where necessary. The 'point fifties' in the P-51D were very dependable if well maintained. We had Tech Orders (maintenance manuals) which were supposed to detail cause and remedy of any problem we ran up against but when we did have a problem it was often one the Tech Order didn't mention.

On one occasion a pilot returned from combat and reported being hit in the right

wing ammunition bay. When the bay was opened it was found that a single round in a belt had detonated but there was no sign of any hit by enemy fire. Armament personnel studied the incident for some time, finally deciding that the round had a sensitive primer and calibration confirmed it had been unusually thin. As the pilot had reported he noticed the incident at the time he was taking evasive action to escape from an enemy aircraft, it was concluded that the ammunition was tossed about in the trays causing the sensitive primer to come into contact with some part with sufficient force to detonate the round. Such a thing was very rare.

An armourer's life was usually very routine but exciting incidents did happen. There was a Berlin show one day (21st March 1944) and when our group returned, Joe Forte—a crew chief—and I happened to be inspecting a kite near the north end of the north-south runway. One Mustang that landed didn't clear the runway and we both noticed that it appeared to be uncontrollable for it started making left-hand circles. We also noticed another Mustang about to land and momentarily disappear from view as there was a hump in the middle of the field which prevented

anyone at the north end of the runway seeing the south end. This also meant the incoming pilot probably hadn't seen the P-51 at the north end. Without saying a word to each other we both ran out to the uncontrollable kite and braced ourselves against the leading edge of the right wing. The pilot gunned his engine and was able to clear the runway just before the landing aircraft passed the spot.

We then discovered the reason for the left-hand turns. A chunk of shrapnel had hit the right side of the plane and penetrated to tear a large hole in pilot Lt. James Dye's hip. Jim couldn't use his right leg on the pedal and therefore couldn't steer his craft off the runway. We signalled the ambulance which came immediately. Jim is a small man and as I lifted him out of the cockpit the blood poured out of the seat of his pants. He was hit near Berlin—400 miles away!

The Germans weren't finished with Dye. He was sent to the hospital at Braintree but a month later there was a night raid during which the hospital was bombed and strafed. Jim was thrown from his bed by the blast of an exploding bomb and broke his leg—the same one that had put him in hospital!

BOXES OF BULLETS
Below left: 'Ole Nick' Nitschke pauses for a picture while unloading belted ammunition at the ammo dump.
Below: Armourers unloading ammunition from a 334th Ftr Sqn P-51D after a mission. Pilot's parachute has been placed on the wing to avoid the possibility of rodents getting inside and doing damage. A parachute was never placed on the ground.

Merlin Mustangs with the RAF

By April 1944 the RAF had received sufficient Merlin Mustangs to establish a second home-based three-squadron wing. Like the first, it was assigned to 2nd Tactical Air Force, the British contingent of the massive assembly of tactical air power being made ready for the forthcoming invasion of the continent. The new wing, No. 133, based at Coolham, Surrey, was composed of one British and two Polish manned squadrons, and like those of 122 Wing they had previously been equipped with Spitfires. The Mustang was immediately popular with pilots; easy to fly, the wide track undercarriage made for safer landings and it had a much more roomy cockpit than their previous charges. Not least appreciated was that aid to pilot welfare, the relief tube: "We were highly chuffed because the Mustang was the first kite most of us had flown in which we were able to have a pee", was the reflective comment of one who had hitherto been sorely troubled by long flights in Spitfires.

With the USAAF now able to meet its requirement for Mustangs to escort the great daylight heavy bomber raids from England, spring found the RAF's Mustang IIIs employed primarily in tactical missions across the Channel, attacking the enemy communication network with gunfire and bombs, but occasionally units would be detached to escort Coastal Command strike forces or fly shipping patrols. In fact, the Mustang's endurance made it an ideal type for this latter work and another squadron, the Polish manned 316, was converted to Mustang IIIs in April specially to afford cover for Coastal Command strike aircraft operating off the Dutch and German seaboard.

From 6th June 1944 the two Mustang wings on the south coast (122 Wing had been moved from Gravesend to Ford) were heavily involved in invasion support operations. On D-Day Plus One, aircraft of 133 Wing, busy inland from the beachheads, were involved in some of the most intense air fighting of the day, destroying 16 Me 109s for a loss of 4 of their Mustangs. During subsequent days both Wings had a number of successful engagements although mainly they were committed to attacking enemy ground forces.

On 24th June, 122 Wing transferred its

sixty aircraft to an airstrip in the Normandy beachhead but 133 remained in England to help deal with the growing menace of V-1 flying bombs, then being directed at London in large numbers from the Pas de Calais launching sites. In July, 316 Squadron was brought down from East Anglia to participate in these defensive sorties and in two months their Poles set the highest score for V-1s shot down by any Mustang squadron—74—before returning to Coltishall.

Shooting down flying bombs was extremely dangerous due to the risk of the bomb exploding when fired at and bringing down the attacker. Several hundred rounds usually had to be expended to bring down one of these small, fast targets and often when ammunition was spent pilots would resort to a fast, close dive in front of the missile to upset its course through the turbulence created. Normally Mustangs could only overhaul flying bombs in a dive as these missiles were often travelling at speeds approaching 400mph. To obtain higher speeds some experimental use was made of the then new 130 octane fuel but this was not entirely satisfactory.

By September 1944 RAF Bomber Command heavies were regularly engaging in daylight raids against targets in western Germany. Fighter escort and support was necessary and to meet this requirement 122

THE OLD MAN LOOKS IN Home of 122 Wing between July and September 1944 was Ellon, an airstrip carved from the Normandy farm lands. QV:I and QV:F of 19 Squadron set out on a patrol watched by Air Vice Marshal Harry Broadhurst, AOC Fighter Command (sitting on the jerrycans), 122 Wing's commander and deputy, Group Captain P. G. Jameson and Wing Commander G. R. A. MacJohnston.

118

Wing was withdrawn from France and based at Matlaske on the Norfolk coast to resume its original role with the Mustang. The following month 133 Wing was also moved into East Anglia, taking up station at Andrews Field, near Braintree, Essex, where it was joined by the Matlaske units and 316 Squadron from Coltishall to form a super wing of seven squadrons. This presented simplified maintenance and supply and also provided concrete runways for the winter months, a facility not available at the Norfolk bases.

With an increasing need for long-range fighters the RAF proceeded to convert six more fighter squadrons to Merlin Mustangs during the last three months of 1944, and in December formed another super wing at Bentwaters in Rendlesham Forest, Suffolk, a station constructed for US heavy bombers but never occupied by them. The expansion of the RAF Mustang fighter force to 250 aircraft during the autumn of 1944 was made possible by substantial deliveries of new machines from the States. These were all Mustang IIIs (P-51Cs) with high fuselage profiles, at a time when the USAAF in Europe had largely re-equipped its combat squadrons with the new 'bubble' canopy P-51D model. This is explained by the fact that Dallas production of the high profile fuselage model continued for a few months

after the Inglewood plant had changed over to the P-51D. Over a third of the total Dallas production was supplied to Britain, mostly later P-51Cs i.e. Mustang IIIs.

While the Mustang III had less firepower than the P-51D its all-round performance was superior due to lighter loadings. And as all Mark IIIs were modified to receive Malcolm hoods before being issued to squadrons the advantage in visibility offered by the P-51D was not all that superior. Like American pilots those of the RAF considered the Me 109 their most difficult adversary in close combat. Indeed, in dog fights some pilots came to regret they were not flying Spitfire IXs when the Messerschmitt showed it could out-acccelerate and out-climb the Merlin Mustang at low altitudes. Equally matched, however, the Mustang III had a much superior performance to the Me 109G.

FOLLOW-MY-LEADER
This view of two 19 Squadron Mustangs IIIs clearly shows how the blown Malcolm hood bulges out from the clean fuselage lines. Despite this the curve of the hood maintained a smooth airflow and, strangely, it was found that performance was actually slightly enhanced. Malcolm hoods were installed on aircraft of 19 and 65 Squadrons at Gravesend in February 1944 and thereafter to new aircraft before delivery to a unit. RAF Mustang IIIs originally had white noses, wing and tail bands as type identification markings but those on the tail were discontinued after March 1944. Note how foot access to the cockpit has worn paint from the left wing root.

JIG SAW PUZZLE
This mangled wreckage was once KH521,5J:I of 126 Sqn., a Mustang III which took part in several operations over Germany and had chased Me 262 jets. Shortly before noon on 9th June 1945, F/O K. A. C. Wright and KH521 engaged in mock combat with USAAF P-51s over East Suffolk, finally breaking away in a dive to return to home base, Bentwaters. Eye witnesses saw parts of the tail come off at about 300 feet and the Mustang hurtle into the ground near Hell Corner, Campsea Ash. F/O Wright should have been killed as he did not have sufficient height for his parachute to open when clearing the aircraft. Miraculously his hurtling body was slowed by the foliage of trees and hedges and he was picked up in a field dazed but with no serious injuries. KH521 was sent to RAE Farnborough and there the tailplane fracture that precipitated the crash was located.

The RAF's Air Fighting Development Unit ran an exhaustive test with a captured Me 109G-6 and a late production Mustang III. The altitude for maximum performance from the Me 109G's Daimler Benz DB-605A engine was 16,000 feet but at this height the Mustang was 30mph faster in level flight and its advantage rose to 50mph at 30,000 feet. The 109 had a slightly better rate of climb up to 20,000 feet but from thereon the Mustang gained a slight advantage. When Zoom climbed (using the inertia obtained in a dive to boost the speed of ascent) there was no appreciable difference in their respective rates. There was little to choose between the two aircraft in rate of roll, though in turning manoeuvres the Mustang could always out-turn the 109. In a dive the Mustang III could draw steadily away from the 109G. Firepower of the Messerschmitt was much heavier than its adversary, three 20 mm cannon and two 13 mm machine guns, but the aircraft lacked endurance having only about 90 minutes under combat conditions. The 109 pilot also had very restricted visibility from the cockpit.

A similar trial with a FW 190A showed the Mustang to be nearly 50mph faster up to 28,000 feet, increasing to 70mph above that height. There was little difference in rate of climb and a slight advantage for the Mustang in turns. The FW 190 was always out-dived by the Mustang but the German fighter had a vastly superior rate of roll.

Of course, there were many variables such as fuel and ordnance loads that could tip the scales in favour of one fighter type or another in actual combat, and this accounts for the contradictory reports on the Mustang's prowess. Enemy interceptors, like those of the Allies, were constantly being improved and the performance of the various sub-types of the Me 109G met in battle improved towards the end of hostilities.

The two Fighter Command Mustang stations, Andrews Field and Bentwaters, each with over 120 aircraft, were the main source of RAF long-range fighters for the remainder of hostilities in western Europe. Their principal duty was escorting Bomber Command heavies to the Ruhr and targets involving deep penetration into hostile airspace, so that these Mustangs were denied the opportunities for engaging enemy interceptors on the scale of their more numerous allies venturing to the far corners of the Reich. Consequently, escort missions were more often than not uneventful in respect of contact with the enemy although in the final six months of the war the Luftwaffe often exhibited a predilection for attacking the British heavies where poorer defensive armament and looser formations made the Lancasters and Halifaxes easier targets than the Fortresses and Liberators.

On 12th December 1944, when 88 Mustangs from Andrews Field provided cover for 140 Lancasters flying to bomb a steelworks at Witten, a mass attack from above by 40 to 50 Me 109s was suddenly made on the bombers. The Mustangs engaged in combat, claiming five of the enemy plus two probables for the loss of only one of their number, but the enemy's tactics downed some of the bombers. It was 23rd March 1945 before Luftwaffe jets made a concerted attack on an RAF Bomber Command formation. Bentwaters Mustangs were then on hand to see 15 to 20 Me 262s come rapidly in on the flank of a Lancaster force bombing a bridge at Bremen. The Mustangs immediately dived on the jets but the enemy's superior speed enabled them to evade with the exception of one aircraft which did not vacate the area quickly enough. F/O A. Yeardley of 126 Squadron was able to get in a well aimed burst after which the Me 262 was observed to dive into the ground. This was the first known jet victory achieved by an RAF Mustang.

The Andrews Field and Bentwaters squadrons were more successful on 8th April when three of the twin-jets were claimed during an attack by an estimated 20 Me 262s on Lancasters bombing Hamburg. Two days later while on an escort to Leipzig RAF Mustangs had their only brush with the Me 163 rocket fighters. One that attempted to dive away was overhauled and shot down by a Bentwaters pilot, F/O Haslop of 165 Squadron.

In February 1945 a third RAF Mustang wing was established in the general East Anglian area at Hunsdon in Hertfordshire, although it never operated more than two squadrons before the end of hostilities. It was the Hunsdon wing that received some of the first Mustang IVs, the British designation for the 'bubble' canopy P-51D and K which eventually began to reach the RAF late in 1944. One of the Hunsdon squadrons, No. 153, was disbanded after only one week's operations with the Mustang (disposing of two FW 190s during this time) its aircraft then being turned over to a Canadian Squadron, No. 442 the Caribous. At VE-Day there were 16 RAF Merlin Mustang squadrons in the UK with some 320 aircraft, still only a small force compared to the US Eighth Air Force's 1600 at that date.

The Poles

THE LEGENDARY HORBACZEWSKI

Right/Centre: Of his 13½ victories, 5½ were achieved while flying Mustangs. The four swastika markings on PK:G indicate four flying bombs brought down. The stories of his personal courage were many, the most notable being the occasion when he landed on an uncompleted Normandy landing strip, rescued one of his pilots who had crashed in a nearby marsh flew him back to base in the Mustang sitting on his lap. Horbaczewski led 315 on many successful scraps, the last two weeks after this picture was taken when the squadron caught a Gruppe of Me 109s and FW 190s assembling near Beauvais. Sixteen enemy aircraft were credited destroyed but the occasion was saddened because the only aircraft missing was Horbaczewski's. No one saw what happened to him; but it is known he had been unwell and insisted on flying even though friends tried to deter him.

Above/Top: Stanislaw Skalski talks to his mechanic while the armourer checks the rounds left after the operation from which 133 Wing's commander has just returned to Ford. Skalski was one of the most successful Polish fighter pilots as the score board on SF:S shows, although most of these victories were obtained with Spitfires and Hurricanes.

SHOWING THE COLOURS
Left: Rolling along the perimeter track at Andrews Field, a section of four 316 Squadron Mustangs display the colourful nose markings that were adopted by some RAF Mustang squadrons in the closing months of the war. The red and white stripes used by 316 were derived from the Polish national colours.

DISPERSAL POINT CHAT
Below: Two pilots of 309 Squadron in front of their Mustang IIIs. Parachutes were not usually laid on the ground; there was always a risk a mouse might take refuge with disastrous chewing results.

SHOWING HER OFF
Left: General Anders, C-in-C Polish Forces, is given a demonstration of what four Point Fifties will do at the Andrews Field butts. This was on the occasion of his visit to the Polish fighter wing at that base on 6th March 1945. The Mustang III jacked up for demonstration is the personal aircraft of Group Captain Tadeusz Rolski and carries his initials TR; a common practice on the personal aircraft of high ranking RAF officers.

123

Toppling a Diver

Tadeusz Szymanski

The Poles flying with the RAF were a gallant and tenacious band. 'Tadek' Szymanski was one who found his way to England in 1940 and saw out the war as a fighter pilot. On his first combat mission his squadron, 316, had its initial encounter with FW 190s and 'Tadek' distinguished himself by being the only pilot to shoot one down—and shared the squadron's amazement at this inaugural feat! Much of his operational experience was in Mustangs and while flying these he sent down nine V-1 flying bombs, a record that made him one of the top five 'Doodlebug' aces flying Mustangs. Two of these V-1s were elbowed out of the sky in a spectacular way.

'Diver patrols'—the code name for the flying bomb defensive sorties—were usually very monotonous, involving flying backwards and forwards over the same little area of the Channel for two hours or more with no contacts. Sometimes the Germans made mass launchings of Doodlebugs to saturate the defences and if you were lucky enough to be flying then, things were far from dull. Such a day was 12th July 1944. In the afternoon I set out from West Malling with my wingman for a Diver patrol 25 miles south of Dungeness. When we reached the area I pushed the radio button to contact our radar controller. He asked me to make a 90 degree turn left then a 90 degree right and finally called, "All right, I've got you". This meant he had identified us on his radar, our abrupt changes of direction helping him to pick us out from any other blips he had on the screen. These radar stations were actually in caravans on the coast, one of them controlling three sections of our squadron. The fellows operating them were so good that many times they would congratulate you for shooting down a Doodlebug before you had time to report it—they

had seen it disappear from the screen.

We were soon given a vector for a flying bomb coming into our area on course for Tunbridge Wells. I picked it up, went into attack, and shot it down. You had to hit them from dead astern and not get closer than 300 yards otherwise you might be brought down by the thing exploding. This meant you were presented with a very small target and on average, it took several hundred rounds to bring one down. Also you had to catch them on the first attempt because they were going so fast—370 to 400mph—if you had to climb for another go you could rarely catch them again. You see, we had to overhaul them in a dive even though the engines of our Mustangs had been specially modified to give us maximum performance at about 5,000 feet. This was done at Coltishall before we moved down to the south coast. Normally the superchargers gave us top speed at 25,000 feet but we needed it at lower altitudes, the Doodlebugs usually came over at between 2,000 and 8,000 feet. Apart from modifying the superchargers, manifold boost was increased from 61 inches to 81 inches for using the new 130 octane petrol. All this was quite a job with many problems. One of my friends was testing a modified engine when it blew up over Coltishall and he had to bale out.

Shortly after I shot down this bomb, radar called again and said, "We have another one for you", giving me course and direction until I spotted it. I called my wing man and said, "Now you can see it— it's in front of us—you get it." But there was no answer from him. I thought he was behind, flying with me, so I called again but he still didn't reply. Looking round he wasn't to be seen so I assumed his radio had packed up and he had gone back to base. Getting behind the Doodlebug I started shooting and saw strikes before my

Warrant Officer Tadeusz Szymanski examines the dented wingtip of his Mustang III, FB377, SZ:R after toppling a V-1 on 12th July 1944. His score of nine V-1s earned him a commemorative plaque from his squadron.

ammunition was finished. The bomb had slowed down, so I called the radar and asked them to send somebody nearby to finish it off but they said, "We haven't got anybody." So I thought perhaps I would go and have a close look at it because we had never seen one from close range. Coming up in close formation—just a few yards away—I got a good look. The thing was jerking along and the elevator was flapping with each vibration of the crude jet motor. I noticed there were no ailerons and also that on the front of the bomb was a silly little propeller. It looked ridiculous, we didn't know at the time but this was the unwinding device set to dive the bomb into the ground after so many miles.

While I was looking at it I remembered an incident when the squadron was resting at Hutton Cranswick in Yorkshire. I had a very good friend, Poldek Sakrzewski—a lovely fellow, he was killed later in Canada—and we did a lot of aerobatics together. On this occasion we were flying Spitfires at 20,000 feet in beautiful still air; it was exhilarating. I called to him and said, "Poldek, I would like to brush your wing tip with mine", just for fun. So I did and he said "Tadek, I could feel the air lifting my wing tip." Then he did the same thing to me and I also noticed the slight lift. With this in mind I decided to try and tip the Doodlebug up with my wing tip. We had been told that its flight was controlled by gyroscopes. If you turn a gyroscope more than 90 degrees it goes haywire so I thought if I could tip the bomb up it might go out of control and crash.

As soon as I put my port wing under the Doodlebug's wing it started lifting. I let it straighten itself out then I put enough of the front part of my wing tip under its wing tip, taking care to keep my aileron out of the way, and then by a sharp bank to starboard I hit it with the port tip. Of course, this put me into a bank to starboard and by the time I could turn back into position to take another look at it, it was flying with the port wing down but gradually straightening itself out. It had lost some height I suppose because it was climbing again. I repeated this manoeuvre eleven times but each time it went over so far and then came back. Just before reaching the balloons, near London, I said to myself I have to get it down so I tried a slightly different manoeuvre hitting very hard with my wing tip as I went up just like into a loop. When I recovered from the manoeuvre to my dismay the Doodlebug was flying perfectly straight and level. Then I suddenly realised the engine was now underneath: I had turned it upside down! I could also see it was gradually going into a dive and then down it went.

A similar thing happened on 6th August but over the sea. I shot one down about 15 miles south of Hastings and shortly after spotted another. I called my wingman and said, "You get it." I was flying line abreast with the bomb and I could see him shooting and pieces flying off the Doodlebug but he used up all his ammunition. By this time we were approaching the coast at a point where we could not cross without being fired on by anti-aircraft guns. So I said, "I'll finish it" and went in, but a few bursts of fire and my ammunition was finished. The Doodlebug was damaged and going slower. So I pulled alongside and gave it a heavy swipe with my wing tip as I pulled up. First time, over it went and down. This was four miles south of Hastings and as I watched it go down I noticed some sort of warship below. For a moment I had the horrible thought that the bomb was going to hit it. Happily it didn't and as we circled I could see the crew waving and cheering. They had a grandstand view. It made their day and mine!

Tadeusz carries off the damaged tip removed from his Mustang after the second incident. He was careful to use only the forward part of the tip. Another Pole who tried toppling a V-1 hit and jammed his Mustang's aileron, went out of control and was killed in the resulting crash. It was a hazardous business and officially wasn't encouraged but some pilots used the technique successfully.

During the final year of the vast conflict of arms in Europe a unique mission fell to Mustang pilots in a little known campaign, described by a participant as 'a sort of separate little war'.

The German occupation of Norway offered a ready base for naval operations against Allied shipping in the North Atlantic and for nearly five years RAF Coastal Command and ships and submarines of the Royal Navy carried on containing actions to prevent, as far as possible, the Germans from pressing this advantage. Due to the rugged nature of the Norwegian terrain, most war supplies coming from Germany, and much needed iron ore going the other way, were shipped along the coast and this shipping was continually harassed from sea and air. To counter RAF activity, the Luftwaffe maintained a force of 50 to 100 interceptors based along the Norwegian seaboard, principally stationed at airfields near the southernmost tip of the country. These fighters had extracted a

DEPARTURE POINT FOR NORWAY
Ten Mustang IVs of 65 Squadron lined up on the Peterhead runway and ready for the 500 mile journey across the North Sea. Each aircraft carries two 108 US gallons 'paper' drop tanks. CO's KITE

Sqn Ldr Peter Hearne retracts the undercart of his QV:J,KM193 20th April 1945. Hearne's comment on his first flight in this Mark IV: "A superb aircraft".

A Separate Little War

heavy toll of slow RAF reconnaissance bombers seeking shipping in these waters, so that later Coastal Command mounted attacks with fast rocket-carrying Mosquitoes and Beaufighters. Even so, the Me 109s and FW 190s often appeared in time to catch the low flying British aircraft and inflict heavy punishment.

With the advent of the Merlin Mustang it was possible to provide an escort of single-seat fighters of equal and better performance to the enemy interceptors en-

countered on the Norwegian coastal strikes. The first long-range escort for Coastal Command by the RAF's Mustang IIIs was in May 1944 and thereafter Beaufighter and Mosquito shipping strikes were rarely without the benefit of Mustang protection. Initially squadrons or flights were sent on detachment from stations in southern England to those on the east coast of Scotland, usually Peterhead, the most easterly airfield on the coast of Aberdeen. Even from here the distances involved in missions to the nearest point in Norway were some 300 miles, but in practice round trips of a thousand miles were not uncommon. While there was nothing spectacular about such vast distances by the spring of 1944 when USAAF Mustangs were regularly making escort missions of twelve hundred miles for a round trip, there was a significant difference in practice. Whereas the American or British fighter pilot escorting heavy bombers flew at altitudes of anything from 20,000 to 30,000 feet, those shepherding a Coastal Command strike force across the grey North Sea flew 'just above the wave-tops'. The element of surprise was particularly essential in anti-shipping operations and to avoid the ever-searching radar beams from German warning stations, the flight out had to be made under cover of the enemy's horizon below which radar could not reach. The journey was treacherous. Every Mustang pilot knew that his life hung on the untroubled running of the "damn great Merlin sticking out in front" for if it quit there was neither time nor height to bale out and if one did survive a crash into the icy sea the chances of survival were small. In winter a man could not live in those freezing northern waters for more than a few minutes.

The danger of flying low over the sea—and such graphic statements as, "Forced to increase altitude due to spray breaking over the aircraft" in flight reports leave no doubts about it being low—was compounded by the monotony of a 2 to 2½ hour flight where a moment's careless relaxation could mean a plunge into the waters below. It was SOP to trim the Mustang to fly slightly nose up, to lessen the chances of flying it into the sea. Sometimes, when weather was bad and cloud overcast hung low, it was "like being in a grey sandwich and trying to fly up the slice". The appearance of the Norwegian coast was greeted as a wonderful sight and brought mental relief—despite its hostile associations. Frequently the weather would open up on approach and in the crystal clear atmosphere the mountains of Norway were a sight most beautiful to behold.

Long range flying technique was to use low engine revs and high boost to conserve fuel. This caused plugs to carbon up and to clear them the policy was to open up the engine every 15 minutes or so.

From rendezvous with the strike force—usually around Fraserburgh—the Mustangs would fly with one or two 4-plane sections on each side of the strike force. On approaching the Norwegian coast the strike force would climb to two or three thousand feet to launch their attack, while the Mustangs went up to five thousand to be above them. Return flights across the North Sea were always at a safer altitude from which it was possible to bale out.

Initially only single squadrons were detached to fly on these missions and the escort rarely totalled more than six to twelve Mustangs. As air combat generally took place below 5,000 feet the adversaries were more evenly matched than usual, the Mustang's performance supremacy being best exploited at twice this height. In consequence the RAF fighters did not always have it all their own way particularly when challenged by numerically superior enemy forces. The principal German fighter organisations were IV and V JG5, fighter Gruppen with some 30 FW 190As and 50 Me 109Gs. Norway was, comparatively, a quiet backwater of the European war, and Lister received many battle-weary but highly experienced Luftwaffe fighter pilots for short periods. It was the nearest thing to a rest unit that many of these men would experience. Additionally JG102, an operational training wing, had training fields for fighter pilots in Norway, and towards the end of hostilities this organisation was often involved in interception. So the calibre of the German pilots encountered might range from the novice to the very proficient.

One of the most successful actions off Norway was that involving the tenacious Poles of 315 Squadron who, led by the legendary Squadron Leader Horbaczewski, claimed 8 of 16 enemy aircraft encountered on 30th July 1944. The majority of the combats—occasionally fought out beneath the towering cliffs of a fjord—were less fruitful and sometimes the Luftwaffe won the day.

In early August, when the RAF Mustang squadrons were heavily committed on the continent and with anti-Diver patrols, the US Eighth Air Force took a hand. On the 8th the elite 4th Fighter Group took a

Beaufighter force on a successful shipping strike and afterwards one squadron strafed Stavanger Sola airfield. The Germans used the rocky terrain to good advantage in shielding parked aircraft and defensive gun emplacements, with the result that the attack proved very costly for the Mustangs with questionable results. Three of the strafers were lost and the pilot of another, Major Leon Blanding, badly wounded by shell fragments in the body and head. The blood bespattered canopy of his Mustang indicated his desperate state and fellow pilots flew on each side of the damaged aircraft to guide it back to Britain. For 300 miles Blanding retained consciousness and through sheer willpower brought the Mustang safely into Acklington. After that no one ventured to strafe the Luftwaffe's Norwegian strongholds.

Contests between the Peterhead Mustangs and the JG5 Focke-Wulfs and Messerschmitts over the narrow strip of water between Denmark and Norway, increased during the final months of the war. With more Mustang squadrons available, the RAF deployed two at Peterhead early in 1945; in fact, the original Merlin Mustang squadrons, 19 and 65. Squadron Leader Peter Hearne took No. 19 to Peterhead and remained in command for the rest of hostilities. He had considerable experience on Mustangs having been with 65 Squadron when it became the first RAF squadron to receive the Merlin version in December 1943. Rejoining the squadron for a second tour in September 1944, he was given command of the 'sister' squadron the following January.

No. 65 saw a lot of action on the Norwegian escorts. On 9th February twelve of its aircraft tangled with an equal number of FW 190s attempting to thwart Beaufighters rocketing two ships off Kristiansund. For the loss of one Mustang, two FW 190s were shot down and two others so badly damaged their pilots had to bale out. Lt Linz, an ace with 70 victories, fell in this fight, probably to the guns of F/Lt Jimmy Butler. A week later, while Mosquitoes were after ships in a fjord southeast of Alesund, nearly 500 miles from Scotland, 14 Me 109s with a top cover of FW 190s hove in sight. The Messerschmitts (of 10/JG5) went for the Mos-

quitoes and 65 Squadron intercepted, claiming three destroyed plus a probable without loss to themselves. For some reason the top cover did not interfere and had disappeared when the engagement was over.

On 12th March, 19 Squadron took 44 Mosquitoes to the Skagerrak. Fog prevailed and as the squadron withdrew they were suddenly jumped by 10 Me 109s of 13/JG5 which shot down a Mustang. Peter Hearne, by his 'Gyro' gunsight and an expenditure of 160 rounds of ammunition, despatched one of the assailants in a turning fight. But 65 still seemed to run into most of the action. On 25th March both squadrons were out and 65, with its new Mustang IVs, engaging between 20 and 30 FW 190s, made claims of three destroyed and two damaged, but lost their CO, Squadron Leader Ian Stewart.

After an uneventful escort for Beaufighters blasting vessels near Lindesnaes, at the southernmost tip of Norway on 11th April, 19 Squadron was flying low over the coast, homeward bound, when Peter Hearne spotted four Me 109s orbiting the airfield on the Lister peninsula. He immediately took a section of Mustangs to intercept but the enemy were not to be surprised and began a steep turning climb. The Mustangs followed, one stalling and almost spinning into the sea, while another pilot, finding his gunsight inoperative, also had to abandon the combat. The Messerschmitts appeared to be outclimbing the Mustangs, so Hearne broke away, followed by his No. 4, and headed as if for home. Then, after flying some 20 miles out to sea, he made a 180 degree turn back to the vicinity of Lister. As he had anticipated, the 109s were circling the airfield and one unwary pilot, apparently Leutnant Adolf Gillet commander of 16/JG5, was despatched into the sea. This combat left Hearne with some respect for his adversaries, for on return to Peterhead he commented: "The 109s we encountered were obviously a highly experienced bunch of boys. Their turning circle is decidedly better than ours at low speed. The lowering of 20 degrees of flap may just enable us to hold them in the turn although I feel they could then out-climb us."

In the four and three months respec-

BEST OF LUCK
A two-finger salute from a fellow officer speeds a 'silver' 65 Squadron Mk IV on its way from Peterhead. This squadron was the first RAF squadron in the UK to be re-equipped with the bubble-canopy Mustang.

tively that 65 and 19 Squadrons were at Peterhead for 'the run to Norway', the former was credited with 14 enemy aircraft destroyed and eight probables for the loss of three in combat, while 19 had three confirmed and a single probable.* All three of 19's confirmed victories were the work of the CO, Peter Hearne, and the last of these was a memorable engagement as Hearne's combat report shows:

"After covering the last of the Beaufighters out over the coast from Josing Fjord I led the Sqn. eastward to sweep around Lister at 5,000 feet while I took my own section of 3 a/c and Green section of 2 a/c inland at 5,000 feet until I came to Fede Fjord. I then turned SW, losing height to zero feet down the fjord and flew as low as possible over the water with Lister airfield in full view on our left. I observed one aircraft airborne over Lister flying very low in a westerly direction. He was, in fact, beating

*Luftwaffe records show this 'probable' to have been a 'destroyed'. F/Lt Jimmy Butler (who transferred from 65 Sqn.) was the victor. Butler was killed when his aircraft was hit by small arms fire while leaving the Danish coast during the operation of 5th April.

up the aerodrome because he pulled up to 400 feet over his base, turned very steeply right (emitting a trail of black smoke) and headed due north for the hill just N of Lister. Here he turned port and put his wheels down intending, I think, to come straight in to land. He had to cross out to sea in this orbit and I intercepted him about 1½ miles off shore NW of his base. As I turned port to intercept him, climbing to 500 feet, a heavy five-gun battery from the shore placed five very accurate flak bursts just in front of me. I identified the e/a as an Me 109 and attacked it from the port quarter with a large angle off; but saw no results. The Me 109, once aware of the situation, pulled his wheels up and gave an amazing display of combat flying, which had he been luckier might have ended disastrously for one or even two of our aircraft. Although heavily outnumbered and with a reasonably good chance of bridging the 1½ miles of sea and seeking the protection of his heavily defended base, he chose to fight it out to the last, firing on every single occasion he could bring his guns to bear. I damaged him slightly in my second burst as a thin trail of white smoke began to issue from his port wing root. I

130

then broke off and circled above him while other Mustangs eager to kill, pounced on the 109. None of them could get sufficient deflection on him until, choosing an appropriate opportunity, I came down on him in a tight turn to port and at an angle of about 70 degrees, I fired a short burst from 200 yards. I saw a red glow appear in his cockpit and he rolled gently over and went vertically into the sea, no more than 1½ miles from his base and in full view, no doubt, of flying control he had been beating up a few moments before in so spectacular manner. This e/a had the usual light grey camouflage with black and white spinners similar to the two other 109s I have encountered from Lister."

This was the final engagement between the Peterhead and Lister antagonists although shipping strike operations off Norway were carried out until the last days of the war in Europe. It was also Sqn Ldr Peter Hearne's fifth victory in a Mustang and one he would always remember for the courage of his opponent.

Pilots of 19 Squadron—and the Medical Officer, extreme right—at Peterhead in April 1945. The CO, Sqn Ldr Peter Hearne is fourth from the left. On his right is one of the flight commanders, Alan Shirreff, a distinguished cricketer. Another well known figure in the post-war world of sport was rugger international Bob Weighill, standing third from the right. The black and yellow ring nose marking adorned all 19 Squadron Mustangs during the last six months of the war.

Banging About by the Med

The Merlin Mustang came to RAF squadrons in the Mediterranean theatres in March 1944. No. 260 Squadron, a unit of the Desert Air Force that had been operating Kittyhawks for many months, was selected to receive the first Mk. IIIs. The squadron was then based at Cutella in Southern Italy and the pilots were flown to Casablanca to collect their new charges. Morris Curteis, a veteran Kittyhawk pilot, quickly dropped any misgivings he had about the change. "It didn't take me long to appreciate that this was a really beautiful aircraft. If it had any bad flight characteristics, handling features or mechanical shortcomings they were so insignificant compared with those I had encountered in other aircraft that they were hardly worth the mention." After a few hours' familiarisation flight Curteis joined others from his squadron in flying the Mustangs from Casablanca to his base, a thousand mile trip.

The initial sorties with the Mustang saw 260 continuing its work as a fighter-bomber unit supporting the ground forces in their difficult struggle through Italy. There were some escort and patrol operations but ground attack predominated. In July 260 was joined by 112 Squadron, its Mustangs resplendent with the famous shark's teeth marking, and by 213 Squadron which moved up from Egypt.

In September another unit that had earned fame in the earlier fighting in Malta and North Africa, 249 Squadron, received Mustang IIIs. The South African Air Force's No. 5 Squadron converted the same month and Royal Australian Air Force's No. 3 re-equipped with Mk IIIs in November. Towards the end of the year all six squadrons, based on the Adriatic coast, came more and more to engage in operations over the Balkans and Aegean. Like Norway, this was a battle of containment, to tie down German forces in the area, with the additional duty of aiding internal liberation forces, principally Yugoslav partisans who were gradually gaining control of large areas of their country.

In their ground support and interdiction missions RAF Mustangs often carried 1,000lb bombs on the wing racks. This was a considerable load to lift from the short rough landing strips on which squadrons were usually based in Italy. To aid take-off stability the fuselage tank was restricted to 40 gallons when it might have appeared

**RIGHT BLOODY
PRIMITIVE, MATE!**
Right: Armourers of 260
Squadron assembling rocket
projectiles on the sands of
Cervia near the Adriatic
coast. Empty wooden
ammunition boxes serve as
work benches and a tarpaulin
keeps the small parts from
falling in the sand. At least
out in the open you could
draw on a fag while putting
fins on rockets. Mustang in
the right background is F/O
'Taffy' Williams' HS:Z.
A DOG'S LIFE
Far right: 'Laddie', 260's
Alsation mascot prefers the
shade even if the steel
planking is a bit hard on the
rear. LACs H. Smith (left)
and J. Tate fix rockets to the
launch rails ready for an
afternoon strike. Ground
crews much preferred handling rockets to bombs as the
former were light enough
for one man to carry. To
keep grit out of engine
exhausts stacks have plugs.
The abrasive grit also
removed paint from prop
blades.
HELPING TITO
Centre: LAC L. Doyle and
Corporal R. Wyer prepare to
fit a 110 US gallon tank on
AK:E of 213 Squadron being
readied for an operation
over Yugoslavia.

more prudent to keep to the manufacturers' recommended limitation of two 500
pounders for the Mk III. Nevertheless, the
RAF carried thousand pounders as routine,
causing some raised eyebrows among their
Allies. On one occasion, as W/O Ronald
'Willie' Williams prepared to take off from
Iesi so loaded his mechanic implored: "Be
sure and get off, Taff." Puzzled by this re-
mark, Williams deduced that his ground
crew and some visiting American airmen
had placed bets on the ability of the Mustang to become airborne with two 1,000
pounders. Williams did 'get off', somewhat
incensed at his life being made a gambling
point!

Considerable trouble was experienced
with bombs hanging up on the wing pylon
shackles of Mustangs. Not infrequently a
bomb would fail to release and could only
be dislodged by violent manoeuvres.
These difficulties resulted from manufacturing deficiencies with individual bombs
and bomb hooks and the trouble was never
completely overcome. On 21st February
1945 a South African pilot flying with 112
Squadron, Lt. R. W. Strever, had to return
to base early due to engine trouble. He
attempted to jettison his bombs at sea but
both stuck fast. Hoping that they were
wedged tightly on the shackles he came in
to land, but the jar on touch-down dislodged them and the resulting explosions
blasted the Mustang 200 yards up the runway and left it a flaming, mangled wreck.
Strever managed to quickly extricate himself and though severely burned on hands
and face he walked to meet the ambulance.

The air-to-ground rocket projectile was
a much favoured weapon with the RAF in
the Mediterranean theatre in low altitude
attack due to its hitting power and accuracy in comparison with bombs. Early in
1945 260 Squadron received the rail equipment for an installation on its Mustangs
allowing up to eight projectiles to be carried. Once the delivery technique had been
mastered, the new weapon soon became
very popular with pilots. Aimed by the
gun-sight a high degree of accuracy was
achieved, particularly against transportation targets. The 60lb warhead of the rocket
had the hitting power of a six-inch shell
but the most pleasing thing to pilots was
that the overall weight of eight projectiles

and launchers was under 600lb, making it
much easier and safer to operate from
short landing strips than bombs. The angle
of attack for dive bombing was 60 degrees,
with rockets on defended targets 45 degrees, and on undefended targets 30
degrees.

Although the six gun Mustang IV arrived in the theatre during the closing
months of the war most of the aircraft employed by the Italian based RAF squadrons
were IIIs like those in Britain. For ground

strafing forays with machine guns the Mk III lacked fire-power although the RAF found it quite adequate for the long-range interdiction of enemy communications in the Balkans. Losses were mainly due to ground fire faced during low level missions but they never rated as high as those in north-west Europe. Nevertheless, the operating conditions and the type of operations saw a lot of Mustangs get 'banged about' but they stood up to it remarkably well. As 260's Morris Curteis put it: "Good solid design and construction that would put up with a lot of punishment."

Contact with enemy aircraft was rare at this stage of the war in the Mediterranean theatre, so much so that Allied pilots sometimes unconsciously assumed that every aircraft they saw during a mission was friendly. On 11th January 1945 a formation from 260 Squadron carried out a dive bombing operation on an Italian rail target over which there was extensive cloud. South African Raymond Veitch was piloting an early Mustang III which, because it did not have a fuselage fuel tank to provide the necessary endurance for the mission, was carrying a drop tank on one wing rack and a 500lb bomb on the other. For control reasons the drop tank had to be released before bombing but at first it stuck fast and was not dislodged until after the rest of the squadron had attacked. Thus delayed, Veitch bombed and proceeded to climb to where other Mustangs were reforming.

Three aircraft were flying ahead of him, just below the cloud base and he was joining up with these when the startling realisation came to him that they were not Mustangs but Me 109s. Veitch immediately prepared to attack the rearmost Messerschmitt which had begun a slow turn to the left.

"It was a beautiful and easy kill, but I had to throttle back so much to get on the tail of the Messerschmitt, who was turning so gently, that I became suspicious and looked over my shoulder—there was no rear-view mirror—to see the 30mm cannon in the nose of an Me 109 lining up on me. I exclaimed, 'Hell! I'm surrounded by Messerschmitts' and instantly lowered flaps, gave the Mustang all that it had, climbed into the cloud and saved my life.

"The Messerschmitts had obviously seen me coming to join up with our squadron. What they'd done in actual fact was to leave a sucker behind in a slow turn, while the others went into steep turns to come in on my tail.

"As I was gazing down that 30mm cannon, it seemed that all the planes in the country were asking where the Messerschmitts were—my exclamation had been heard over the radio. At that moment I wasn't very interested in their troubles!"

After a few minutes' searching the area and with silence from Veitch, the leader of 260 Squadron called up: "Hello, Kenboy Blue 2. Have you been shot down yet?" "No,

135

Right: Mustangs of 260 Sqn. in a victory fly past over Campo Forimido, near Udine on 28th May 1945. The three 'silver' Mk IVs do not have rocket rails.

Above/Right: K 25 cameras mounted in the wings of 260 Sqn Mustangs took excellent photographs of targets attacked with rockets. Farm buildings occupied by German troops before and after an attack by F/Lt Bobby Brown and Flight: 12th April 1945.

I'm in a cloud," came the relieved reply.

The irrepressible Raymond Veitch—nicknamed 'Dronkie'—had more 'lives' than the proverbial cat. He was to feature in a remarkable series of escapes that is probably without parallel.

On 2nd April 1945 he was flying wingman to F/Lt R. S. 'Bobby' Brown in the lead of a formation of ten rocket-laden Mustangs. The squadron found and attacked a large column of motor vehicles between Maribor and Strasz in Yugoslavia during which a bullet fired from the ground must have started a glycol leak in Veitch's aircraft. After firing his rockets Veitch reported engine overheating to the

leader who detailed another Mustang to escort him back to base at Cervia in Italy. Climbing to 7,000 feet they had just crossed the west coast of the Istrian peninsula when Veitch's engine overheated to such a degree that it failed and caught fire. Veitch immediately lowered the flaps, stood on his seat and jumped towards the trailing edge of the wing. This took him clear of the Mustang and he floated down on his parachute into the sea about four miles west of a small coastal town. Meanwhile the pilot of the escorting Mustang radioed Air Sea Rescue and orbited Veitch's dinghy until a Walrus amphibian arrived overhead. Much to Veitch's puzzlement and annoyance the Walrus circled continuously overhead making no attempt to effect a rescue. Two Mustangs arrived to keep watch and eventually a Warwick appeared and dropped a lifeboat by parachutes. This landed 50 yards from the downed pilot who once aboard found a disturbing but explanatory note for the reluctance of the Walrus to land: "Steer course out to sea; Walrus will pick you up. We suspect mines in this area."

The lifeboat, rather large for one man operation, was eventually got underway, but not before another boat observed pulling out from the shore towards Veitch had been warned off by a burst of fire across its bows from a patrolling Mustang. No mines were seen and having progressed a few miles out to sea an American Catalina arrived on the scene and landed. On board Veitch was given a swig of Chianti and flown direct to his base to make a triumphant return wearing sealskin boots and ornate maroon pyjamas.

Two days later 'Dronkie' Veitch returned from operations with 20mm cannon shell damage to his aircraft. Next day, 5th April, he set off in another Mustang again flying No. 2 to F/L Bobby Brown and again the glycol system of his aircraft was hit by ground fire; this time during an attack on a train in Kamnik station. Brown despatched another Mustang to shepherd him home but the damaged engine was overheating badly and by the time they had reached the coast north of Trieste it ceased. Veitch glided down to about 6,000 feet and baled out in the same way as before. Climbing into his dinghy he could see hostile shore was only about two miles away so he commenced paddling out to sea. An enemy motor torpedo boat put out from Trieste but a watchful Mustang attacked it with rockets and caused it to withdraw. Two Spitfires and a Catalina arrived but were fired on from the shore. Additionally, it appeared that our hero was once again in the middle of a large minefield so that the Catalina was forced to withdraw and a Warwick with airborne lifeboat was called. Veitch kept paddling westwards with a constant fighter umbrella above him.

In the afternoon a sail boat approached. Squadron Leader Peter Blomfield, CO of 260, who at the time was keeping an eye on Veitch, twice warned the vessel off with bursts of fire across its bows. Then he observed that the four occupants in dark uniforms were firing revolvers at him and as they continued towards Veitch he had no option but to destroy the boat. No survivors were seen. The Warwick arrived in the late afternoon but no sooner had Veitch gained the lifeboat that it dropped, than a 40mm gun started firing at him from the shore. Taking a weaving course he managed to escape any hits although some rounds hit the sea ten yards away. By the time the firing ceased he had travelled some twelve to fifteen miles. The Catalina reappeared but Veitch was still in the minefield so it was unable to land. Following course directions from those above, the lifeboat continued out to sea, but when darkness fell and the escort departed Veitch stopped the boat's engines so that any enemy vessels that might be abroad at night would not detect him. At dawn Squadron Leader Blomfield was back to exchange a spirited two-finger salute with the occupant of the lifeboat. Still positioned in a minefield, some further hours sailing were necessary before a Catalina could land and take Veitch off. Once inside the flying-boat he was greeted by a crewman with, "Haven't I seen you before?" It was the same American crew that rescued him three days before.

On 30th April Veitch was flying another armed reconnaissance during which road transportation was attacked at Udine. A missile, believed to have been debris from his rocket attack, hit an oil line in his Merlin which began to lose lubrication pressure. At 7,000 feet the engine seized and 'Dronkie' repeated the now familiar baleout procedure but this time he banged an arm on the tailplane. Once again he found himself in a minefield about five miles offshore from Lignano. After spending the night in his dinghy he was again the recipient of an airborne lifeboat. Luck held and he managed to escape the minefield where he was met and taken in tow by an A/S/R launch. After this third adventure it was suggested by his superiors that a special rescue flight be assigned to watch over his personal fortunes. But the war was all but over.

R. H. VEITCH
The invincible South African who always made it back to base even if his Mustang didn't.

Mustangs Against Japan

The first Merlin Mustangs to be flown against the Japanese were shipped into India early in 1944 to sustain units equipped with the Allison versions. By April the 311th Group at Dinjan, near the Burma border, was adding P-51Bs to its collection of P-51A and A-36A models, while a few were assigned to the 1st Air Commando Group. The three tube 'Bazooka' rocket clusters were, initially, not installed as they aggravated the centre of gravity problem associated with the P-51B and C fuselage tank and had dangerous effects on handling qualities. There was unanimous enthusiasm in this theatre of war for the enhanced performance of the new Mustangs, especially from China where Major General Claire Chennault, commander of the USAAF's 14th Air Force, clamoured for all he could get. Long range was a paramount requirement in carrying the war to the enemy in that war torn land where hostilities covered some two thousand miles. At that time, however, the bulk of Mustang production was flowing to the forces in Europe which had priority and not until the end of 1944 were sufficient Mustangs available to satisfy the needs of units in the CBI. By then the 23rd and 51st Fighter Groups had completely converted to Merlin Mustangs and the 311th Group had moved up from India in an exchange deal for one of the China-based, shorter ranged, P-47 groups. This made a total of ten Mustang squadrons with over 250 aircraft in China by the end of 1944.

Practically all maintenance supplies were brought into China by air, including aviation fuel carried and stored in 40 gallon barrels. Rust from these containers was a frequent problem in aircraft fuel systems, until a crude but effective filter was devised for use when filling tanks. Maintenance facilities were primitive to the extreme, yet with the aid of local Chinese labour and commendable improvisation a high rate of serviceability was achieved and sustained. The Mustang force in China was called upon to perform a variety of combat roles but most frequently ground strafing and bombing attacks against transport, particularly in attempts to thwart the Japanese advances made during the latter half of 1944. Neutralising airfields was an important task at which the 311th Group had much success. From September the 14th Air Force stationed P-51s at an advanced base at Hsian, in an isolated Chinese held area in the north, to attack enemy airfields and communications along the Yellow River area, hitherto fairly immune from such disturbance.

Due to the limited amount of fuel available at Hsian only one squadron of the 311th was in residence at one time. The Group adopted the nickname Yellow Scorpions, a description originally bestowed in a derogatory Japanese propaganda broadcast on the demise of the yellow-nosed Mustangs of the Group's 530th Squadron. It was this squadron that made some particularly successful strikes against the major Japanese airfield in this part of China.

On 22nd December a flight of Yellow Scorpions on a high altitude sweep spotted a great many aircraft parked on an airfield at Tsinan, a large northern city. The squadron usually operated with two 500lb bombs on ground attack strikes, but Tsinan was too far from Hsian for bombs to be carried. So, with the aid of two 110 US gallon drop tanks a dozen Mustangs paid a surprise visit to the airfield on Christmas Eve. Finding little in the way of anti-aircraft defences, they strafed the field for half-an-hour leaving an estimated 39 Japanese planes burning. Two days later they were back and set fire to 29 more, but a third visit on 3rd January was met with intense ground fire which holed several Mustangs and caused the squadron to vacate the scene of action after adding 13 more parked aircraft to their score. Not only had the Japanese moved in anti-aircraft defences to deter their antagonists, but on this occasion a dozen Oscars were sent to intercept. Some smart evasive action and bluff dog fighting followed, as all but one of the Scorpions were out of ammunition, but by using their superior speed all eleven Mustangs were able to escape without loss.

Similar attacks on Japanese airfields and communications were carried out by the relieving sister squadron, the 528th, taking over in February 1945. For a year a score of Mustangs had been the principal factor in restricting Japanese activities in the northern provinces of China. The versatility of this long range fighter-cum-bomber-cum-ground-attack aircraft made it the most prized piece of equipment in the 14th Air Force's arsenal.

In addition to the Mustang force active in the dusty Chinese plains, another was established early in 1945 to provide better all-round fighter capability against Japanese interceptors encountered in the South-West Pacific Area war zone. Here the Allied offensive which had begun at the eastern end of New Guinea in 1943 had progressed north-west from that hot and humid land to liberate the Philippine Islands. Two veteran fighter groups—the 35th and 348th—were re-equipped with P-51Ds in March 1945, but the first Mustangs to arrive were P-51Ds of the 3rd Air Commando Group (formed to emulate the behind-the-lines technique successfully developed by its namesakes in Burma) and F-6D camera-equipped models to replace the ageing P-40s of the 71st Reconnaissance Group. It was during an early Mustang operation by a pair of aircraft from this

organisation that a unique combat with enemy fighters occurred.

Captain William Shomo and 2/Lt. Paul Lipscomb were the pilots of two photographic Mustangs on low-level reconnaissance of enemy airfields in North Luzon on 11th January 1945. Nearing the area of their objective Shomo saw a formation of enemy aircraft approaching them about 2,000 feet higher. The Jap formation was identified as a Tojo and Tony fighters escorting a single Betty bomber; the strength of escort suggesting some important personage in the Betty. In such a situation, where the enemy had the advantage in height and numbers, Shomo would have been in order ignoring them and continuing on his mission. But as the enemy displayed no intention of attacking the two Mustangs Shomo reasoned they had either not been seen or had been mistaken for friendly types—the Mustang being new to that theatre. He led Lipscomb in a climbing curve so that they positioned themselves behind the enemy machines and slightly above before attacking. Shomo opened fire on a Tony which immediately exploded. He then side-slipped to avoid overshooting and put a burst into another Tony with similar results. This rude awakening alerted the other Japanese fighters to meet their attackers but one turned in front of Shomo and a short burst sent it down. Lipscomb had meanwhile destroyed two other fighters. Shomo then made for the Betty giving it a well-aimed burst from underneath and sending it down in flames. He then found an enemy fighter coming towards him head-on—firing first he sent this down too. Gaining sufficient altitude to clear his tail and turn, Shomo saw some of the remaining fighters below and dived after them. Sending one down in flames, he continued his dive to pick off a fleeing Tony only a few hundred feet above

141

IN TIGER GARB

Below: The Mustang became a must in China, and no one was more enthusiastic about its prowess than Colonel 'Tex' Hill (pictured) who commanded the 23rd Fighter Group of Flying Tiger fame. This weather-beaten P-51B was one of the few Merlin Mustangs acquired by the group at Kweilin in the summer of 1944.

PICKIN' HER BONES

Right: Flying Tiger's yellow banded P-51C '259' was in need of repair but the part wasn't available in China. So items were borrowed to keep other Mustangs flying and before long there wasn't much left of '259'. Chinese workmen at this air depot stripped the airframe to make a reserve of spares.

BLACKED OUT TIGERS

Right: 'Nok-Out' leads three other P-51Ds of the 75th Ftr. Sqn., 23rd Fighter Group over a typical Chinese backcloth of flooded rice paddies. The date is 1945, gone are the famous 'tiger teeth' noses, a black empennage being the group identification marking. Black, white and yellow were the predominant colours used to mark aircraft flying from China. Red was taboo as this was the colour of the Japanese 'meatball' insignia.

142

PAPPY

Top: Highest scoring fighter ace in the CBI was John Herbst who was credited with shooting down 20 Japanese aircraft between July 1944 and February 1945. He had previously flown in North Africa and when he came to the 23rd Fighter Group to command the 74th Ftr. Sqn. he was 34, about ten years older than the average age of pilots in his unit. The slogan 'Tommy's Dad' identified his personal Mustang—the one above is P-51B 43-7060—and brought him the nickname 'Pappy' from his more youthful pilots. A mixture of chance, audacity, keen eyesight and quick reaction brought Herbst his run of successful combats at a time when Japanese air opposition was waning in China. Like a number of other top aces he was killed in a flying accident in the immediate post-war years.

NETTED

Above: The shining unpainted P-51Cs that arrived in India in the spring of 1944 were thought too conspicuous to park uncloaked on forward airfields. A fine net was used to hide the glare and break up the outline of 42-106528 of 529th Ftr. Sqn., 311th Group.

Iwo Mustangs

SUN SOAKED

It took some of the bloodiest fighting of the whole Pacific war to wrest the island of Iwo Jima from the Japanese. In March 1945 when Mustangs arrived there was little space for parking but as enemy air attack was unlikely the fighters were lined up together along the 'ash' runways of Central Field. Most of the 70 odd aircraft of the 21st Fighter Group's three squadrons appear in the photograph above. Taxying had to be performed with minimum power to avoid whipping up too much dust with the slipstream. The pilot's seat on the D could be raised to give a better view although it was necessary to have the canopy back. Even so forward visibility was still restricted by the Merlin and the pair of blue banded P-51Ds of the 46th Ftr. Sqn. (lower picture) are manoeuvred gingerly.

144

the ground. By the time he had regained altitude the other Japanese fighters had disappeared. Shomo had destroyed seven—a record for action against the Japanese on a single sortie—and Lipscomb three. For his performance Shomo was later awarded the Medal of Honor, the only such decoration to a Mustang pilot versus Japan.

This action took more than audacity. It again illustrates the vulnerability of the armourless Japanese fighters to a brief burst of well-aimed fire and the measure of confidence US pilots had in their aircraft and tactics at this date. The Merlin Mustang could outpace the Tony and the Oscar in level flight, but its angle and rate of climb were not so good, and it could not compete in slow level turns. The light and nimble Japanese fighters were ideal for dog fighting but were lost in dealing with the speed pass—the 'old one-two' tactics evolved by US pilots flying the inferior Bell P-39 and Curtiss P-40 back in 1942. This was standard technique in air fighting with Japanese interceptors, but with its superior performance the Mustang was able to employ these tactics with much greater effect. If a leader and wing man kept together and did not make 180 degree turns within range of their opponents, they could command the fight simply by making straight through passes and avoid a turning fight. Even so, providing speeds were kept above 350mph in a turn a Mustang was reasonably safe from being outmanoeuvred by Japanese fighters.

A third Mustang force in action against the Japanese was created to provide an escort force for B-29 Superfortresses established in the Mariana Islands during 1944. The Marianas lay some 1,500 miles southeast of Japan providing good launch points for bombing attacks against industrial and military targets in the enemy's homeland. Bases much nearer to Japan were required for long-range fighters to escort the B-29s and in February 1945 the island of Iwo Jima, some 660 miles from Tokyo, was invaded to obtain suitable sites. Japanese opposition was formidable and the occupation of the island was only achieved with appalling casualties.

Two fighter groups, the 15th and 21st, were sent to Iwo Jima in March 1945. The 15th moved into the south strip early in the

145

BUNKER BLASTERS

Below: In May 1945 Mustangs went to war against Japanese island strongholds in the Boni group with 5 inch rockets carried on neat pylon installations that did away with the cumbersome rail or tube launchers. Five of these missiles could be carried under each wing but as the two inboard sets of pylons were close to the bomb rack only three rockets could be carried under each wing when drop tanks were in place. Aimed with the gunsight and fired by pressing a button on top of the control stick, these weapons were much preferred for ground attack although to achieve accurate hits much practice was required. The armourer is fusing the rockets which the pilot will arm through a solenoid in the forward pylon before firing. The cobra insignia is that of the 78th Ftr. Sqn.

FOX HOLE FILLER

Bottom: Two 500 lb bombs were the usual load for a Mustang but two 1,000 lb bombs could be carried subject to flight restrictions. The bombs were armed electrically and released by the stick button after a switch selection. The 15th Fighter Group armourer is tightening the sway brace to prevent the bomb from oscillating during flight.

DUSTY DEMISE

Above/Right: A take-off run through the dust created by a previous take-off caused these two 21st Fighter Group Mustangs to crash off the end of the strip. Volcanic dust choked air filters and starved of air the Merlins cut out. 'Honey Chile' took fire but her injured pilot was rescued. The other aircraft did not burn despite coming to rest on its punctured drop tanks. These pictures give a good impression of the battle blasted state of Iwo Jima.

SAFELY HOME
Far left: Despite having lost a large part of its tailplane to anti-aircraft fire, this 45th Ftr. Sqn. P-51D was able to make a successful landing on Iwo. The armed guard was one of many posted in case Japanese troops came out of hiding in the island's caves.

DUSTY DEPARTURE
Left: Getting a formation assembled was a slow process as it was necessary to let the dust settle after each element had left the runway at North Field. P-51Ds of the 506th Group's 485th Ftr. Sqn. wait their turn for an escort mission to Japan that may last six or seven hours.

fences until 7th April when each of the six squadrons despatched four four-plane sections to escort a large force of B-29s assigned to bomb the Nakajima aircraft factory outside Tokyo. Involving a round trip of almost 1,500 miles, near the maximum range of the Mustangs even with two 110 gallon drop tanks per aircraft, there was no margin for navigational errors as the time the Mustangs were able to spend over Japan had to be limited to the critical time when the B-29 force was going in to bomb. To ensure the Mustangs were on time a non-bomb carrying Superfortress led each group on the long over-water flight to a point off the coast of Japan. The shepherding B-29s then orbited until the Mustangs returned from the target area, to navigate them home to Iwo Jima. During the target approach several Japanese interceptors were encountered and though they were able to down one B-29 and one Mustang, the 15th and 21st Groups made counter claims of 21 destroyed. A third Mustang group, the 506th, joined the two other groups on operations from Iwo Jima in mid-May.

The Mustang faced an uncongenial environment in the central Pacific. Iwo

month while fighting was still in progress and for the next few days supported ground troops by strafing and bombing enemy positions. By the middle of the month another airstrip in the north-west of the island was ready to receive the aircraft of the 21st Group. Three nights after their arrival, Japanese infantry secreted in the caves of the rocky island's hills penetrated the 21st camp area and killed as many of the Group's personnel as they could find. The attack was beaten off with heavy losses to the Japanese but there were 44 fatal US casualties and twice that number of wounded.

Notwithstanding this bold attempt to annihilate them, the 21st flew its first mission the following day to bomb and shoot up enemy troop positions on a neighbouring island. Both groups continued chiefly in a ground attack role, neutralising island de-

Jima's airstrips were built from blasted and ground volcanic rock; the abrasive dust whipped up by drying winds played havoc with engineering and maintenance work, and particularly with sensitive carburettor air intakes. In some cases clogged air filters choked engines on take-off causing crash-landings on the rocky surfaces beyond the runways. It was necessary to stagger take-offs to give time for the dust created by each run to settle.

Weather conditions were also hazardous and the violent summer storms that brewed up over this part of the Pacific had to be avoided. The turbulence within some thunderheads would tear the wings from a Mustang in seconds. Weather reconnaissance aircraft usually flew ahead of the Mustangs on the long hauls to and from Japan, but even then the weather could spring a sudden trap. It was a weather front that brought the heaviest loss of Mustangs on any mission during the Second World War.

On 1st June 1945, 148 Mustangs set out to escort B-29s on a mission to southern Honshu. A vast cloud front threatened but the take-off could not be delayed if the Mustangs were to meet their schedule.

Half-way to their rendezvous the formations were engulfed in clouds towering four or five miles high from sea level. At 20,000 feet, with no sign of breaking through, some formations returned to base. Chaos reigned in the clouds as aborting formations flew through and into others with a series of collisions that brought 27 Mustangs down from the sky with only five of their pilots surviving. Formations amounting to 29 aircraft did break through the cloud front and flew the mission. This staggering loss had a dampening effect upon morale in these groups and it was some days before all units could be brought back to full strength. A regular air sea rescue patrol during long range missions to Japan saved the lives of many Mustang pilots who had to bale out over the sea after action over the mainland.

The 1,400 mile round trips to Japan were some of the longest missions undertaken by Mustangs. Pilots spent eight hours and more in the air and the monotony of the long over-water flights and confined conditions of the cockpit brought many fatigue problems. Nevertheless, the Mustang asserted its supremacy over Japan as it had elsewhere in hostile airspace.

UNIQUE SCOREBOARD
Far left: For a pilot to sport victory symbols for the three Axis powers on his personal aircraft was unusual enough, but Cpt. Louis Curdes' P-51D, 44-63272, had a Stars and Stripes as well. It was not a joke; Curdes shot down a US aircraft during his service with the 3rd Air Commando Group. While returning from a reconnaissance in the Philippine Islands his wingman had to bale out and Curdes circled the pilot in his dinghy while a rescue party was awaited. During his vigil a Douglas C-47 transport appeared and was seen lowering its undercarriage and preparing to land on an enemy held island. Despite its US marking Curdes reasoned that it might be enemy operated as no friendly transport should be in a hostile area. He therefore carefully shot up each engine so the transport was forced to ditch, all twelve occupants escaping. It was later discovered that the C-47 was US operated but had been hopelessly lost and out of fuel. His action had a lighter side as one of the two nurses on board was a girl-friend. Curdes' German and Italian victories were achieved while he was flying P-38 Lightnings in North Africa.
TOO LATE
Left: The RAF planned to make extensive use of the Mustang IV in the Burma war zone during the latter part of 1945. Several hundred were shipped to India but the war ended before they entered combat. About 350 were scrapped on the assembly field. KM735 (alias P-51D 44-64712) was one of these assembled and tested at Dum Dum airfield, Calcutta. Rocket projectile pylons can be seen under the wing.

–and War Again

SPRINGBOK
CONTRIBUTION
Mustangs of No. 2 Squadron,
South African Air Force,
lined up for 'R and R'
(Rearm and Refuel) at
Pusan, August 1952. Korean
armourers are loading a
dented drop tank filled with
Napalm on to a jockey
trolley prior to installation
on an aircraft.

When Japan capitulated in August 1945 the USAAF had approximately 5,500 Mustangs on hand while the RAF and Commonwealth air forces held another 1,300. A renowned fighter, it found a ready market with the air forces of many nations during the immediate post-war years, the US Government disposing of between six and seven hundred in this way. Gradual disbandment of the RAF complement saw the last squadrons in Italy and the UK withdrawn by January 1947. In America interceptor squadrons received the P-51H but the new jet fighter, the Lockheed P-80 Shooting Star, soon replaced them in regular air force units. Air defence of the USA in peace time was backed up by a second-line force of squadrons manned by the 'part time' personnel of the Air National Guard (ANG). Between May 1946 and December 1948, 28 ANG squadrons received 700 surplus P-51Ds—or more correctly F-51Ds, the USAF having substituted the letter F—Fighter for P— Pursuit in 1948. Four squadrons with a tactical reconnaissance mission later received RF-51Ds, the redesignation of the camera-equipped Mustangs after the F system of designating photographic mission aircraft was discontinued. F-51H models were not received by the ANG in large numbers until the early fifties when regular USAF units in the States relinquished them for jet fighters. All told, 68 of the 98 ANG squadrons were operating Mustangs at the peak early in 1952. Thereafter, modern jet aircraft were increasingly available and the last ANG unit converted from Mustangs in the summer of 1955.

Surplus USAF Mustangs, less their armament, could be purchased for as little as $3,500 each during the late nineteen forties. Several air racing enthusiasts bought these machines to modify for use in the revived National Air Races and other competitive events. Their performance was improved by eliminating items of military equipment, increasing engine power by over-boosting, and streamlining refinements such as fairing over gun ports. The well known sporting and film stunt pilot Paul Mantz was a Mustang devotee who won the first post-war cross-country Bendix air race at an average speed of 435 mph; moreover, the top four places were taken by Mustangs and it is notable that first, second and third were P-51C type models which had the edge in speed over the later D and Ks. The 1949 Bendix was won by Joe DeBona in another P-51C type, extensively modified and with an ultra-high standard of finish. His average speed was more than 470mph, the highest recorded for a Mustang in any competitive event. Mustangs continued to be raced for a quarter of a century although age and caution limited the speeds. To enhance streamlining some of these racers featured lowered and smoother cockpit lines and there were even attempts to reduce radiator scoop area. A few examples had radiators mounted in faired metal containers at each wing tip; one of these stalled and crashed during the 1949 National Air Races causing three fatalities—including the pilot. Thereafter, the authorities were more restrictive on air racing as it appeared that many enthusiasts were modifying aircraft to a point where they endangered the lives of pilots and spectators alike.

When in August 1945 North American's Dallas plant ceased production of the P-51, on the other side of the world the Commonwealth Aircraft Corporation's factory at Port Melbourne, Victoria, Australia was commencing production of licence-built Mustangs. Arrangements for the manufacture in Australia were completed early in 1944 and components for the assembly of 100 of the P-51D type were shipped from

Inglewood that year. Designated Mustang Mk 20s, they embodied most of the US factory refinements by the time they reached squadrons in the spring of 1946. Eighty aircraft were produced from the US made parts, followed by 120 constructed from Australian components as Mk 21s with Packard engines and Mk 23 with British-built Merlins. Twenty-eight aircraft modified for camera work were designated Mk 22. The Australian-made Mustangs served chiefly with the RAAF wing on occupational duties in Japan during the immediate post-war years. Some Merlin Mustangs had been sent to Australia from the USA during the latter stages of the war in the Pacific, but not seeing action were used to equip two Royal Netherlands Army Air Corps squadrons, Nos. 121 and 122, which subsequently moved into the Dutch East Indies. During the troubles with Indonesian Nationalists these Mustangs were constantly in action and when Indonesia was established as an independent state the Mustangs were among aircraft turned over to form the nucleus of the new nation's air force.

Mustangs from disbanded USAAF formations were supplied to Chiang Kaishek's forces engaged in civil war with the Chinese Communists and some of these were flown to Formosa when the Nationalists had to vacate the mainland.

During the decade following the Second World War Mustangs were operated by the air forces of Sweden, Italy, France, Switzerland, Israel, Canada, New Zealand, the Philippines and most of the Latin American States—Dominica, Honduras, Guatemala, Cuba, Uruguay, Nicaragua and Haiti. A few turned up elsewhere, for during the immediate post-war period the Mustang was undoubtedly the most popular fighter with the smaller national air arms. This largely passive period was short

lived and when, on the morning of 25th June 1950 the North Koreans invaded South Korea, the Mustang was once again involved in a full scale war.

Although the success of the Communists in China had left an uneasy peace in the Orient, the Korean War found US forces unprepared for the conflict to which they were soon committed. The USAF had three fighter groups of three squadrons each on occupational duty in Japan, another fighter group in Okinawa and a fifth in the Philippines. All were being re-equipped with F-80 Shooting Stars but this had not progressed far although 365 F-80s had been sent to the area. There were also three all-weather squadrons of some 30 F-82 Twin-Mustangs. While this was more than sufficient to deal with the meagre North Korean air force of obsolete propeller-driven Russian-made types, the F-80s were handicapped in the vital ground attack role because of their poor duration and a need to operate from long, hard-surfaced runways. Luckily, over 100 Mustangs were at Tachikawa, Japan, waiting to be scrapped at this date; they were in fact scheduled to have been broken up by June 1950 but an officer there delayed this action by various means because he 'had a feeling' it was not prudent. So when the war broke there was a ready-made reserve of fighters available to meet the deficiencies of the jets. Additionally, 145 Mustangs were shipped from the western United States soon after hostilities commenced. The Communist offensive pushed the South Korean and US forces back to a defence line around Pusan on the southern tip of the Korean peninsula followed by a US counter-offensive in September 1950 that saw the UN forces advance into North Korea until the Chinese entered upon the scene in November and the battle moved south once more.

The first air action of the Korean War involved a few Yak fighters attempting to harass air traffic at Kimpo Airfield near Seoul, the South Korean capital, and five Twin Mustangs of the 68th Fighter Squadron. This action, on 27th June, resulted in three of the Yaks being shot down. Thereafter the Twin Mustangs were generally restricted to the air defence of Japan and Okinawa before being replaced by jet types during 1951.

Mustangs used in the Korean War were almost exclusively late D models fitted with pads for mounting six rockets under each wing. The P-51H model, too light for fighter-bomber work, was not employed in Korea. The Mustang was considered superior to the F-80 and later jet types in ground attack duties through its ability to manoeuvre at slower speeds, giving better opportunities to observe ground targets particularly when under direction of front line controllers. The mountainous terrain of Korea made fighter-bomber work ex-

tremely difficult, and very hazardous for the pilot quickly seeking a suitable spot to crash land a damaged aircraft. The old glycol hazard was again to prove a major cause of Mustang loss and one such incident brought the third and final Medal of Honor award to a Mustang pilot.

On 5th August 1950 Major Louis J. Sebille, commander of the 67th Fighter Squadron, led a section of four F-51Ds from Ashiya air base in north-eastern Japan to give close air support to UN forces in the Pusan area. Each aircraft carried two 500lb bombs and four 5in rockets. One Mustang developed mechanical trouble and turned back to base, while the others continued across the Sea of Japan to make landfall near Pusan. Ground control vectored them to the Hamchang area where enemy forces were crossing the Naktong river. Sebille attacked enemy troops on a sand bar in the middle of the river, but one bomb stuck and would not fall despite all attempts to dislodge it

OLD PLANES FOR NEW
Right: Royal Australian Air Force's 77 Squadron traded its Mustangs for Meteors at Iwakuni, South Japan in February and March 1951. Part of the occupational air forces in Japan when hostilities broke out in Korea, No. 77 was soon in action flying its first operation —an escort for USAAF Invader bombers—on 2nd July 1950. Subsequently, like the USAAF Mustang squadrons, it was committed to the dangerous ground attack mission and lost two COs amongst its casualties. The Meteor, alas, was obsolete as an interceptor and could not be profitably used for ground attack.
SURE WAS RUGGED
Far right: An inhospitable backdrop of clouds and mountains that was the Korean environment of the Mustang. The flight line of the 18th Fighter Bomber Group hums with activity despite the lengthening shadows of evening. A crew chief runs up an early P-51D that had originally been despatched to the Pacific for an earlier war.

154

by manoeuvres. Sebille then joined the other two Mustangs in strafing attacks during which they spotted a number of enemy vehicles hidden under trees on the west bank of the river. While attacking these with rockets the Mustangs came under small arms fire and as they circled round the target area, Captain Martin Johnson noticed Sebille's aircraft was streaming engine coolant from its radiator, so he called him over the radio. There was no coherent reply at first, but after warning Sebille a third time Johnson heard the Major say, "They hit me". Johnson suggested he fly south-east to reach the UN base at Taegu but Sebille replied, "No, I am going to get that bastard." Making a tight turn under Johnson's Mustang, he headed in a shallow dive towards the targets previously attacked. He was seen to open fire with his guns and fly straight into a vehicle. There was an enormous explosion as the remaining bomb and rockets still unfired were detonated. It was pre-

sumed Major Sebille had been fatally wounded when hit by ground fire. That his final gesture was a deliberate action is beyond doubt.

The Mustang took the brunt of the ground support operations during the first year of the Korean War and in consequence losses were high in comparison with other Allied fighter types involved. Of the total of 194 P-51Ds lost during the war only ten are known to have been shot down by enemy aircraft while all but twelve of the remainder positively succumbed to ground fire. By the late summer of 1951 only one USAF group was still operating Mustangs, the 18th Fighter Bomb Group with No. 2 Squadron of the South African Air Force attached, but it continued to do so until January 1953 before converting to jets. However, Mustangs operated by USAF-trained South Korean pilots were in action to the final days of the conflict in the following July. To simplify operation and maintenance, tailwheels on their aircraft

were locked in the down position.

With the Armistice of July 1953 the only remaining USAF Mustangs in Korea were those of the 45th Tactical Reconnaissance Squadron which had been organised in September 1950 for duties over the battle lines. Mustangs continued to serve with the Air National Guard in the United States for a few years and the last machine, 44-74936 from 167th Fighter Squadron, West Virginia, was presented to the US Air Force Museum at Wright-Patterson, Ohio in March 1957, where it remains on permanent exhibition.

With surplus USAF Mustangs again available for sale in the USA, a number were purchased for private flying during the late fifties and early sixties. Two-seat conversions to a design by Trans-Florida Aviation of Sarasota, Florida, were per-

SMILIN' THROUGH
A direct hit from a 40 mm shell tore this hole, over two feet wide, in the port wing of an 18th Fighter Bomb Group aircraft while attacking enemy ground positions. "I thought an earthquake had hit me," was pilot Lt. Walter Burke's comment.

mitted in 1959 and this company subsequently produced a large number of these conversions of P-51D and Ks for civilian use under the Cavalier label. The company eventually changed its title to Cavalier Aircraft Corporation, specialising in Mustang conversion. During the nineteen sixties over 100 two-seat Mustang conversions were built.

In February 1967 the USAF placed a contract with Cavalier for 15 two-seat versions of re-built P-51Ds. These had an addition to the height of the vertical tail to improve stall characteristics, reinforced wing spars to support a maximum of one 1,000lb bomb and six 5-inch rockets under each wing. British gun sights replaced the earlier type and modern radio equipment was installed. These aircraft were supplied to Bolivia, Dominica and Guatemala while

six single-seat P-51D re-builds went to Salvador.

As a private venture Cavalier produced a Mustang variant to meet the counter-insurgency role that arose out of initial ex-perience in the Vietnam conflict. Known as Mustang II the prototype flew in Dec-ember 1967. A further reinforced wing enabled a maximum of 4,500lb of under-wing stores to be carried while two 110 gallon fuel tanks for the 1760hp Merlin were permanently attached to each wingtip to give the Mustang II an endurance of 7½ hours. The idea behind the Mustang II was basically to offer the USAF a less costly alternative to developing an entirely new aircraft. Although impressed, the USAF did not place an order. A further Cavalier development known as Mustang III was similar but featured a Rolls-Royce

Dart Turbo-prop power plant to give en-hanced performance. This machine and project was sold to Piper when Cavalier dissolved in 1971 and has apparently not been developed further.

By the 1970s the only military Mustangs still in service were the few mentioned in Latin and South American states where, in one instance, their guns were fired in a show of strength during the overthrow of government. For the most part the hundred or so Mustangs still flying in the seventies are sports or fast business models as tail-ored by Cavalier. Unlike most of its con-temporaries the Mustang still flies in some numbers and is not just a museum curiosity. But then this is only to be ex-pected of an aircraft that was undoubtedly the best all round single-seat fighter of the Second World War.

WHAT A NICKNAME!
The Americans were quick to build up the Republic of Korea Air Force and the obvious choice for its novice pilots was the docile P-51. Five inch rockets were popular weapons as pilots were less likely to get into difficulties than when manoeuvring with a load of heavy bombs. The Allied air forces wrote off 200 Mustangs in combat and nearly as many again in accidents during the Korean War.

157

Korea was the scene of the Mustang's last war in the service of the USAF. An aircraft with a good endurance was required for loitering in the vicinity of the front to attack enemy ground forces. The Mustang was not an ideal choice—a less vulnerable radial engined type would probably have fared better in an environment of small arms fire—but it was available in the war zone and possessed the desired endurance which the F-80 Shooting Star jets did not have. Because of the nature of its employment the Mustang took the highest combat losses of any warplane during the Korean conflict. The mountainous terrain rarely allowed a safe crash-landing and there was little chance of parachuting successfully if an aircraft was crippled by enemy fire at the low altitudes required in ground attack. In consequence two out of three pilots of F-51s lost did not escape from their aircraft. A total of 164 were either killed or missing during hostilities and another 41 wounded. First Lieutenant Robert Dunnavant was one of the luckier Mustang pilots of the Korean War. The story he tells begins in 1948:

I was assigned to the 39th Fighter Squadron, 35th Fighter Group at Johnson Field (Irumagawa), Japan, as part of the Air Force of Occupation. We flew F-51s until early 1950 when we converted to F-80 jets and the Mustangs were flown down to Tachikawa and put in mothballs. We didn't get into the Korean fracas right at the beginning because there weren't facilities for operating our jets near to the battle area. In early July they had a short 5,000 feet strip with PSP planking over-run ready for us at Ashiya (west coast of Japan) and we started flying missions out of there against the advancing North Korean ground forces. After I'd flown 35 missions the F-80s were taken away and we were given

F-51s again. We had some reservations about going back to Mustangs. It was a good aircraft but I guess it was that we felt we had a better chance of survival in the F-80. For a start the jet was much faster and didn't announce its arrival like the F-51 did. As the guns were all nose mounted it didn't present the pilot with the sighting problems that one had with the converging fire from the wing mounted weapons of the F-51. The F-80 also had an air-conditioned cockpit and was more com-

Mustang   Robert Dunnavant

Lt. Robert H. Dunnavant posing before his Mustang a few weeks before the 39th Ftr. Sqn. converted to the F-80.

fortable. True, the jet had range problems —high fuel consumption at low altitude— but we usually had from three to five minutes deck time for ground attack runs on these missions.

With the Mustang on 7th August we moved to Pohang, east of Taegu, in Korea, but in four days the North Koreans had got to within a few miles of the strip and we were forced to move back to Kyushu, Japan. We then operated across the Korean Strait out of a field called Tsuiki,

but often used the Taegu strip, sometimes spending the night there.

While the F-51 couldn't give us the speed of the jets it proved quick to get in and out on a strike and could carry a larger load. We carried varied ordnance; GP or frag bombs, napalm and rockets, in addition to the six 0.50 cal machine guns. The rockets didn't appear to be very effective against heavily armoured enemy vehicles until we got the new 5-inch shaped charge type with which it was possible to stop the

159

T-34 tank the Reds were using. On some occasions we landed on South Korean strips to re-arm and re-fuel and at times assisted in loading and servicing; it wasn't difficult. Although the situation was a bit chaotic at this time squadron morale was good and losses were few. I had confidence in the aircraft and the liquid-cooled engine was the only worry for we knew it was fairly vulnerable. Most of the ground fire I encountered was small calibre or 20mm. On one or two occasions I did see what appeared to be 40mm bursts but mainly the fire was small arms.

My plane took hits on five or six missions but nothing serious until my 35th in an F-51. I took off from Taegu strip on that one on the morning of 12th September. The F-51 was carrying two 500lb bombs and six rockets.

Our flight orbited at about 8,000 feet in an area 20 miles south west of Taegu waiting to be called in by the forward air controller operating over the battle area in a T-6 spotter. We were soon called and vectored to where an enemy troop concentration was supposed to be. The terrain was rugged and hilly but well covered with vegetation. I couldn't locate the target and eventually attacked the pin-point location we'd been given. I dropped the bombs on the first pass and then went in with rockets but two refused to fire. The effect of our attack was probably nil for I didn't see the enemy or any return fire. There was some though, as I found out on my third strafing pass. I was at about 200 feet when suddenly oil burst over the windshield. I assumed the plane had taken a hit in an oil line so I immediately started climbing, at the same time turning south east. The oil temperature was rising rapidly and thinking the engine might catch fire I decided to bale out. With the failed rockets still under the wings a forced landing was out of the question.

At about a thousand feet and with little forward visibility through the oil soaked windshield I released the canopy. Immediately oil streamed round the sides of the windshield, causing my eyelids to stick closed and seriously hampering my ability to see. I stood up preparatory to going over the side but as I did I hit the gun trigger on the stick and the guns started spraying bullets around the hills. I had forgotten to put the gun switch off. The Sutton harness of my parachute had a central buckle locked with a safety pin which I'd failed to put in. When I tried to stand up again I knocked the buckle and all the straps broke loose so I was no longer attached to my parachute! Luckily the plane was still chugging with 140 to 150 IAS and about 1,000 feet altitude. I buckled the harness, retrimmed for hands off flight and scrambled headlong over the side. The slipstream slapped me against the fuselage and I remember seeing things as if in slow motion—the fuselage moving past and the tail section approaching slowly. Then the horizontal stabiliser hit my right leg below the knee and flipped me. The pain wasn't great at the time but I had a sensation of being stopped in mid-air. When I pulled the rip cord there was no jolt, no pull, as if I was already suspended.

About 30 seconds after the 'chute opened I hit the ground. I was looking up at the time and didn't realise how close to the ground I was when the 'chute opened, a good thing as I never had a chance to worry about where I was going to land with my injured leg. I found I had hit on a dirt road, the only one in the area it later turned out, and rolled off into a rice paddy. I then began to feel the pain and one look at my twisted leg confirmed it was broken. My wingman had seen me bale out and flew over and waggled his wings before heading south so I knew help would be on its way. I was pretty sure I was in friendly territory as I had made good and sure that I had come far enough south before leaving the aircraft. I lay there cursing as I watched the wreck of my plane burn about half a mile away. Cursed my luck in being hit, and cursed the controller who put me on to that 'phantom' strike, I was still cursing when the Jeep arrived with a litter to pick me up and take me to an advanced First Aid station not far away.

They sent me back to the States on a hospital ship the following month. I could see the old leg wasn't like it had been; it didn't set quite straight. Guess I'll carry the mark of that plane for life. Doesn't bother me much unless the weather's damp and then it aches a bit. Sort of like having one's own built-in weather clock!